FIRST PEOPLE THEN AND NOW

Introducing Indigenous Australians

Marji Hill

The Prison Tree Press

2021

Disclaimer

All the material contained in this book is provided for educational and informational purposes only. No responsibility can be taken for any results or outcomes resulting from the use of this material.

While every attempt has been made to provide information that is both accurate and effective, the author does not assume any responsibility for the accuracy or use/misuse of this information.

The Prison Tree Press
Suite 124
1-10 Albert Avenue
Broadbeach, Queensland 4218
Australia

Acknowledgements

In the spirit of reconciliation, I acknowledge the traditional custodians of country throughout Australia. I pay my respect to elders past, present and emerging and extend my respect to all Aboriginal and Torres Strait Islander peoples today.

Also, in the spirit of reconciliation my mission is to increase the understanding between Indigenous and Non-Indigenous Australians and to provide people from all over the globe some basic understanding of Australia's first people, their history and cultures.

I would like to thank Sherien Foley for reading and editing the first edition of the manuscript. Thank you, too, Eddie Dowd for assisting with this second edition.

Marji Hill

Table of Contents

CHAPTER 1

Who are Australia's first people?

Australia was one of the earliest centres of civilisation in the world with its beginnings around 65,000 years ago. What was once the unknown continent was inhabited by Indigenous Australians.

Australia's first people then and now were global pioneers in many ways. They were among the first great sea voyagers. Between 40,000 and 100,000 years ago the first people had to cross the waters between northern Australia and the islands of Southeast Asia.

They developed a sophisticated technology making tools and weapons made of stone. They were among the first to practice aerodynamics with the creation of the boomerang.

Indigenous Australians understood the dynamics of land conservation and management and they developed a religious, social and cultural life that recognised the essential bonds between mankind and the land.

In the history of Australia's first people, they demonstrated their ability to reach for the stars in art, in legend and oral history. In their ceremonial life they embraced the first ritual expression ever undertaken in the history of the world and their burial ceremonies pointed to a firmly held belief in the afterlife.

Terminology and definition

Indigenous Australians are made up of two separate groups of people - Aborigines and Torres Strait Islanders. The term

'Indigenous" is used to cover both groups of people but use of this terminology is not without controversy. While "Indigenous Australians" is the current and accepted terminology in government, many Aboriginal people do not like to be called Indigenous. A lot prefer to be known as Aboriginal or Torres Strait Islander rather than being called by the generic term Indigenous Australian.

For the purpose of this book the words "Aboriginal people," "Aboriginal Australians" and "Torres Strait Islanders" will be used.

Prior to 1788 the word "Aborigines" was not used by the first Australians. Aboriginal people used their own names - names that were local to their people because there were over 250 separate and distinct cultural groups in Australia. They still use the names applicable to their own group or nation. It was the British colonisers who gave the name "Aborigine" to the original inhabitants.

While the term Aboriginal or Aborigine applies to Indigenous Australians in general most Aboriginal people prefer to be called by their own group or regional name, such as, Wiradjuri, Gurindji, Pitjantjatjara, Larrakia. Torres Strait Islanders like to be known by their island names such as a Saibai Islander.

Aboriginal people themselves will use terms like Koori, Murri or Nunga to refer to their people or even will use terms like the "saltwater people" or "spinifex people".

If referring to the first Australians as a group the following terminology is acceptable: Aboriginal people, Aboriginal Australians, Torres Strait Islanders, or Indigenous Australians.

Many Non-Indigenous Australians use racist or derogatory words when talking about Aborigines and Torres Strait Islanders. Words that cause offence are "full blood", "Abo," "half caste," "nigger" and "boong".

These words have racist connotations; they are prejudicial; and it is not appropriate to use them.

Many Non-Indigenous people define an Aboriginal person as someone who is a "full-blood" or in terms of the degree of Aboriginal blood they have. This criterion was based on the colour of the skin - like they have no white blood or the degree of white blood that they have.

If an Aboriginal person had a white parent they were classified as "half caste". While historically many thought this way, such classification is now regarded as racist and offensive.

How an Aboriginal person is defined is based on relationships.

Defining Aboriginality rests on three criteria. Australian government policy lists the criteria as being:
- recognised as such by other Aboriginal and Torres Strait Islander people particularly by people from their community
- identifying as an Aboriginal or Torres Strait Islander, and
- being of Aboriginal or Torres Strait Island descent.

Human occupation

Many Aboriginal people believe that their origins lay in Australia - that human beings were created in Australia.

But archaeological evidence is unveiling the story of Australia's first people. The scientific perspective suggests dates for human occupation that may go as far back as 100,000 years.

At least it seems that Australian Aborigines have a continuous history dating back to 65,000 years.

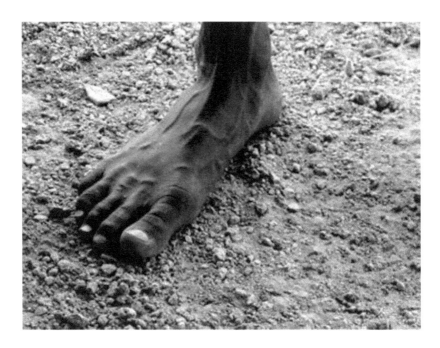

Clear archaeological evidence indicates that Aborigines were living in south eastern Australia 40,000 years ago.

At Lake Mungo in the Lake Mungo National Park in New South Wales a male skeleton was found in 1974. This male corpse, now known as Mungo Man, lived there all those years ago.

Lake Mungo is one of several dry lakes in the World Heritage listed Willandra Lakes Region. Red ochre was found on the skeleton and this discovery indicates that there was some form of ritual practiced at the time.

Pigments such as ochre tell us a lot about the past. Not only does the ochre found on the corpses indicate that there was some form of religious ritual all those years ago but it implies that it was used for art - cave painting, decoration of objects, and body painting. So what was happening over 40,000 years ago is still happening today.

A female skeleton was found at Lake Mungo. Known as Mungo Lady, she has also been dated the same age as the male skeleton and is the oldest cremated human remains that has been found to date.

At Madjedbebe, a sandstone rock shelter, (formerly known as Malakunanja II) in the Northern Territory archaeological evidence indicates that human beings may have been living in this area over 55,000 years ago.

The rock shelter is situated on the western side of the Arnhem Land approximately 40 kilometres (45 miles) west of the East Alligator River.

This means that the site contains the oldest evidence of human occupation in the country, so it makes this rock shelter Australia's oldest site.

Origins

But where did these ancestors come from if they did not originate in Australia?

Scientific evidence is limited and there is a lot of conjecture.

Photograph by Marji Hill

The general consensus among the prehistorians is that the first Australians came to the southern continent via Southeast Asia.

There was some kind of major sea crossing - that's for sure. The question is whether this crossing of the sea was something deliberate or whether it was an accidental crossing. If accidental the first people could have been caught in monsoonal winds - all of this a question still being debated.

The first Australians were among the first sea voyagers. They would have had to travel over water of less than 100 kilometres (approximately 62 miles).

We do not even know what kind of boat or watercraft the first Australians came in. There are no remains of boats, so it is hard for archaeologists to determine the kind of water transport they came in. Whether they came by boat or raft again remain as unanswered questions.

Prehistorians are still not in agreement even as to whether there was one migration of the earliest people or if there were several. There is no conclusive evidence.

Changing environments

Over thousands and thousands of years the first people had to adapt to dramatic changes in the environment. This was caused by climate change and the movement of land masses.

From about 80,000 to 7000 years ago there was an Ice Age which continued to varying degrees of intensity. The sea levels were much lower than they are now, and the land mass of the continent was much greater. Areas of land that are now under the ocean were once home to the early Australians.

The Willandra Lakes region in south western New South Wales was once a rich and thriving environment - flourishing with life. What is today a barren, desert-like, arid environment was

40,000 years ago a place which provided an abundance of vegetation. There were plenty of plant and animal food resources irrigated by a river system.

Volcanoes were active.

There were giant kangaroos, echidnas, koalas and diprotodons. These animals moved over the land, enjoying the lush, tropical jungles and vegetation.

The first people that lived in those ancient times developed social organisations, developed technology, managed the land, controlled plant growth and had a highly developed religious set of beliefs, commonly now known as the Dreamtime.

Information about Australia's past is gathered from the evidence of prehistorians - from the scientific evidence collected from archaeological sites across the continent.

It is possible to piece together what life was like before 1788. A lot of this information has been collected from the accounts of early European settlers and the scientific research of ethnographers of the nineteenth and twentieth centuries.

Population

The 2016 Census estimates that 798,400 Indigenous people were living in Australia with three quarters of the population living in New South Wales, Queensland and Western Australia. This represents 3.3% of the total Australian population.

When comparing the 2016 Census estimates with those of 2011 there is a 19% increase in the Aboriginal and Torres Strait Islander population. It was 669,900 in June 2011.

In 1788 the Aboriginal population was estimated to be somewhere between 500,000 and 1,000,000 people. However, other estimates indicate the population could have been 300,000 to 3,000,000 people.

Archaeological evidence suggests that 750,000 people could have been sustained on the Australian continent in 1788.

Aboriginal and Torres Strait Islander people today live throughout the Australian continent.

Some live in remote communities in particular in North Queensland, Northern Territory, Western Australia and South Australia.

When the Australian Government passed the *Aboriginal Land Rights (Northern Territory) Act 1976* many Aboriginal people left country towns and mission settlements and moved back to their traditional lands.

They chose to go back to their homelands rather than live in the towns.

These small settlements are called "outstations" or "homelands". On these outstations Aboriginal people could return to the old ways of living and revive and revitalise their traditional cultures. They could look after their own country, enjoy its foods and draw strength from its spiritual places.

Estimated Aboriginal and Torres Strait Islander Population in the States - 30 June 2016 (Australian Bureau of Statistics 2016 Census)

New South Wales	265,685
Victoria	57,767
Queensland	221,276
Western Australia	100,512
South Australia	42,265
Tasmania	28,537
Australian Capital Territory	7,513
Northern Territory	74,546
TOTAL	798,365
Torres Strait Islanders	

The Torres Strait is that body of water that separates Australia from Papua New Guinea. It was named after the Spanish navigator, Luis Vaez de Torres, who sailed into the Strait in 1606. The inhabitants of the Torres Strait are called the Torres Strait Islanders.

Four sets of islands make up the Torres Strait. The groups of islands are:

- the western islands which include Badu, Mabuiag, Thursday Island (Waiben), Moa and Muralag
- the central islands, including Yam
- the northern islands, including Saibai
- the eastern islands including Darnley Island (Erub) and Mer

The language and culture of the Torres Strait Islanders are quite different to that of mainland Aboriginal Australians, says Anna Shnukal. Torres Strait Islanders are culturally and physically of Melanesian origin, that is, like the people of Papua New Guinea.

The Torres Strait Islanders speak two distinct languages. In the Eastern Islands (Erub, Mer and Ugar) the traditional language is *Meriam Mir*, while the Western and Central Island groups speak either *Kala Lagaw Ya* or *Kala Kawa Ya*, which are dialects of the same language.

Since European contact a Torres Strait Creole, *Broken*, has evolved from the nineteenth century pidgin English of the southwest Pacific and is now common throughout the islands.

In 1872 and then in 1879 the Torres Strait Islands were taken over by the government of Queensland which had become a new colony in 1859.

By this time, the Torres Strait was popular with the pearlers who worked the shell beds in the strait. Being a large industry in the 1890s it provided cheap labour with the pearlers coming from the South Pacific and Asia.

Missionaries had also arrived. Most Torres Strait Islanders were and still are practising Christians. They followed the Calvinist teachings of missionaries from the London Missionary Society and combined them with their traditional culture. The Coming of the Light festival is held each year, and this celebrates the day the London Missionary Society first arrived in Torres Strait.

The London Missionary Society was officially replaced by the Church of England 1915. The majority of Islanders remained Anglicans until other Christian faiths made their presence on the islands.

In 1982 a Torres Strait Islander called Eddie Mabo together with four other men began a court case to establish their traditional rights over Merian land.

This legal action led to the landmark High Court decision in 1992 which was known as the Mabo court case. The High Court of Australia recognised native title on the island of Mer.

That same year the Torres Strait Islanders adopted their flag which was designed by a fifteen-year-old - Bernard Namok.

Queensland remained in charge of the Torres Strait until well into the 1970s when local governments were established on the islands.

Language

In 1788 the Aboriginal population was divided into more than 250 groups speaking distinctive languages and identifying as social groups which in European countries would have been known as nations.

Aboriginal languages embraced approximately 700 dialects. Just as there are dialects of English so the dialects of Aboriginal Australia varied among themselves. Major languages such as Pitjantjatjara, Bundjalang, Wiradjuri or Gupapuyngu are as distinct as English is to French, German, Italian or Japanese.

Around 120 Aboriginal languages are spoken today. A lot of work is being done by linguists and Aboriginal people to record existing languages and to revive languages that are under threat of dying out as senior people pass away.

Senior Aboriginal people want to preserve their languages as the maintenance, revival and preservation of languages is critical to Aboriginal cultural health. Some of the languages have only a few speakers and there is concern that the languages will die when their speakers pass on.

Recording the languages is not an easy task. It is very important that the surviving languages are kept alive and are passed on to future generations.

Aboriginal and Torres Strait Islander languages spoken in communities today are languages with complex grammatical structures and words, and they have a number of dialects.

Torres Strait Islanders speak a number of languages. Some of them are related to Aboriginal languages while others are related to the languages of Papua New Guinea (islands to the north of Cape York Peninsula).

Many Aboriginal people both in the past and today are multilingual and are able to speak the dialects or languages of their neighbouring people. Some languages are spoken as a first language and are being taught in school.

Some Aboriginal people today speak Aboriginal English - dialects of English. There is no one dialect of Aboriginal English. It can range from being close to standard Australian English to being influenced by Kriol.

Organisations such as the Federation of Aboriginal and Torres Strait Islander Languages and Culture (FATSILC) help maintain and revive the languages that were thought to be dead or forgotten. FATSILC was established in 1991 to promote the maintenance, retrieval and revival of Indigenous languages and culture.

Chapter 2

Aboriginal Religion

Dreamtime is the religion of Australia's first people then and now. All of life and culture originated in the Dreamtime.

Ancestral beings emerged from the subterranean world and moved over a featureless earth.

Dreamtime was that creative time when the great ancestral beings journeyed across the continent and had their adventures. During this creation period the ancestral beings created the universe, the land and its geographical features.

Photograph by Marji Hill

They created the animals and plants. In the heroic Dreamtime sagas, the ancestral beings roamed the country carving out the valleys, the rivers and the mountains.

In their adventures they left behind the caverns, the rocks, the shady pools with their own spirit children.   They left all living things - the people, the plants, the animals, the insects, the fish, and the birds.

Totems

The link between the people and the great ancestral beings are totems. The kangaroo is a manifestation of the Giant Kangaroo and the emu the Emu Ancestor.

Aboriginal people are connected to the land by these spiritual links.

Ancestral beings established the boundaries, the sacred sites and the religious ceremonies that bound people to their obligations to the land and its conservation.

When the great deeds of creation were completed the ancestral beings withdrew into the land. They withdrew to places where they could watch over the land and over the activities of those into whose care they had placed it.

They created an interconnected system of relationships and formulated a set of rules for all to live by. While their presence was hidden, they remained a vital force and retained the power to intervene in the lives of the people that they had created.

Ceremonies were performed to harness the power of the ancestral beings. The creative powers would flow renewing and invigorating the spirit force that ran through the land and through all things that lived in it.

The spirit force gave new life and it strengthened the spiritual bonds which bound people in unity to one another and to particular animals, plants and places with which they shared a common spirit.

Ritual learning

Humans got their spiritual identification from the totems at birth or just before they were born. One or other parent might observe an unusual phenomenon - a goanna standing upright to block the parent's path, a species of fish leaping from the water near the parent, a screeching parrot flying suddenly from a nearby bush.

This will tell the parent the totemic group that the child belongs to. This will be the child's personal totem.

Throughout life that totem will define a whole area of relationship and responsibility to the totemic group who share that totem, to the species of plant, bird, mammal, reptile, fish or insect that is his/her totem and to the spirit from which the totem originates.

Then from their parents they inherit their family ancestry, which gives them rights and responsibilities in both their father's and their mother's family country. From the social organisation of the group that their family belongs to, they are given their social position in relation to those who are not members of their immediate family.

Among other things this tells them who, among these other families, are potential marriage partners. It also defines for them the sorts of relationship they may have with other people in their extended family and group connections. - who can be friends, who they can play with and later work with, and who they must avoid.

Every Aboriginal person has a role to play in contributing to the well-being of his/her family and to the group to which his/her family belongs.

Children have to be taught the proper respect to be shown various members of their immediate family. They must learn the forms of appropriate behaviour that are to be observed with each person in a relationship.

The importance of the parents establishing the child's spirit source, its personal totem, is that it establishes from the very beginning of its life the child's essential being.

It tells where the child's spirit has come from, and where it will return to when it departs its body. It establishes the spiritual responsibilities the child will share throughout its life with those who share its totem.

Most importantly it maps the path the child will follow as it grows to spiritual and social maturity.

That path will take the child through a series of spiritual initiations. These begin at puberty and continue, so long as the person accepts the responsibilities that go with the knowledge that they will acquire.

These learnings continue until their middle and later years when they have become masters of all the law that is theirs to learn. In these initiations what they are is revealed to them step by step.

With each initiation the social and spiritual self which was theirs from the moment of their spiritual conception is unveiled. They learn progressively, as does the community to which they belong, who and what they are.

Each initiation moves them to a higher grade of spiritual and social responsibility. From being minor performers in ceremonial ritual, they become ritual leaders and managers.

They become the elders, charged with watching over the law for their group. The elders are the decision makers, the judges, the peacekeepers, the negotiators, guardians of the group's traditions and knowledge. They are the teachers who see that the young men and women, over time, come to know who and what they are.

But this passing through the fullness of law to attain senior status among their people is not an inevitability. Seniority is the privilege of those who respect the law and accept the responsibilities each new revelation of law brings.

Being yourself then in the Aboriginal tradition means achieving the fullness of the identity that each person possesses from the moment of his/her spiritual conception.

Oral traditions

Aboriginal oral traditions are integral to Aboriginal culture and remain alive today. A lot is being done to record these traditions and to record the stories into written form.

The oral traditions embody the Dreamtime. They tell how the world came into being - the mountains, rivers, rocks, animals, birds, insects, plant life and humans. The oral traditions tell of the sagas of the Dreamtime many thousands of years ago.

For example, the ancestral spirit, Kaaloo, the tiny pure white rat set the waters free to flow in the land of the Gulngai people in North Queensland.

A story about Emu and Brolga from the Nunggubuyu people in Arnhem Land in the Northern Territory tells how Emu is lazy and greedy while Brolga goes to work collecting food. The story tells of the conflict between the two and explains why emus run through the scrub trees and why brolgas have a red patch on their head.

The story of Gurangatch, part-fish and part-reptile, is about the creation of the rivers and valleys of the southern highlands of New South Wales.

Another story is about the ancestral being, Kuniya, the carpet snake, who camped and hunted by a waterhole on a large flat sandhill. In the story the sandhill turned into stone becoming Uluru (Ayers Rock) in Central Australia.

In Western Arnhem Land in the top end of the Northern Territory there are many stories about the rainbow serpent. One is about a rainbow snake called Ambidj which swallowed a lot of people from Goulburn Island. After this Ambidj was chased up a creek and speared to death. The hunters cut open the snake to rescue the people it swallowed. At the place where Ambidj died there is now a big freshwater lagoon which never gets dry.

Other spirit beings beside the great ancestral heroes inhabit the countryside. Some shy spirits live in the dark crevices of rocks and caves or dwell in water holes. Some spirits are mischievous and others are powerful and can intervene in the lives of people.

Photograph by Marji Hill

The ancestral beings travelled across the countryside in the Dreamtime shaping it, planting and peopling the land. Their journeys crisscross the Australian continent. Along these ancestral tracks are sites of special significance where certain events and incidents happened.

All of these adventures happened in the Dreamtime - that time in the far distant past when all the land was flat, empty and dark. The Dreamtime heroes had many adventures creating the world. Sometimes they were destroyed. Sometimes they changed into living forms or into rocks, trees or other features of the landscape. When the creation adventures were over, they disappeared into the earth or sea or sky.

The many places in the land where the Dreamtime heroes disappeared are special places. They can also be dangerous places, because the powers of the Dreamtime heroes can still be felt today.

Photograph by Marji Hill

The ancestral beings remain active, even though you cannot see them. Their anger is to be feared and avoided at all times.

These special places might therefore be dangerous to people who do not belong there. Even people who do belong must take care to warn the spirit of the place that they are coming to visit. These places are the most sacred places in Aboriginal religion. They are very secret.

The story tellers who tell the stories can only tell the story that relates to the country that they live in and own.

Ceremonies

A major story or song cycle is part of ceremonial ritual. A ceremony evokes the power of ancestral beings and encourages them to release again their creative powers.

Great creative sagas are re-enacted in song and dance. Days can be spent in preparation for a ceremony making carvings, paintings, sand sculptures and other ritual items.

There are different kinds of ceremonies.

Public ceremonies are for the enjoyment of men, women and children in which they take part. These are mainly to do with every-day activities such as hunting and food gathering.

There are public religious ceremonies in which everyone can take part. There are religious ceremonies which are partially secret from which women and children are excluded.

Then there are the secret, sacred ceremonies. These are only for initiated men or women. Men have their secret ceremonies and women have theirs. Secret male ceremonies are restricted to men initiated into that particular secret ceremony, and to those about to be initiated into the ceremony.

Women have their own secret ceremonies from which men are excluded.

Many of the ceremonial grounds found in eastern Australia were attached by a path to a preparation ground. When the preparations for the ceremonies were completed the participants moved from the preparation area to the ceremonial ground.

These are called "bora" grounds. They might dance their way there singing verses of the song cycle which belonged to that particular ceremony.

Aboriginal religious ceremonies are a whole complex of dance, song, body decoration, sculptures, paintings and other ritual objects. There are sounds of musical accompaniment, cries, and shouts from the audience, clapping and stamping, flaring torches, sounds and smells.

Those taking part in the ceremony dress up and paint themselves to represent the ancestral beings - animals, people and spirits which form part of the story.

All these elements combined together produce a meaningful and powerful religious effect for everyone present.

Initiation ceremonies

Some ceremonies mark the "rites of passage" marking important stages in a person's life. First initiation marks the beginning of adulthood. This is important because it sets the child on the path to adult knowledge of law and religion. This sort of knowledge cannot be given to uninitiated people.

Ceremonies for male initiation are more elaborate than for girls. Initiation ceremonies for boys occurs around the ages of 10 and 16 years. They must show that they are prepared to respect the law that will be revealed to them and that they will carefully guard the secrets that they will learn.

All of the law will not be revealed to them at their first initiation. Greater revelations will come over time so long as they show themselves to be worthy guardians of the law and its mysteries.

Details of initiation ceremonies will vary from group to group. The main purpose of the ceremony is to mark the changes from childhood to manhood and to emphasise the importance of this change in a boy's life.

While a boy will know that he is soon to be initiated he will not know when exactly. But the senior men know when and where the ceremony will take place.

When the time comes the boys are isolated from the other children and women. The boys are painted and men around them chant the verses of the initiation songs. There is clapping of clap sticks and the stamping of feet as the boys are taken into the ceremonial ground.

The boys may hear the roaring of the spirit monsters made by the twirling bull-roarers. Heads covered they are guided to the ceremonial ground where they must lie flat while the ritual proceeds around them. When the boy leaves the ground, he will be wearing the marks which show that he is now a man.

The boy after seeing his family and relations has to go and live in a young man's camp where he undergoes formal instruction into the law and mysteries. As part of his education he is taken and shown special places in the country for which he now has some ritual responsibility.

He is also taken to places for which other clans, especially his mother's clan, have responsibility. He is introduced to those clans and to neighbouring people as a man with responsibility to them as well as to his own people.

Funeral ceremonies

When a person dies, customs for handling grief vary throughout Australian Aboriginal cultures.

These customs always include marked displays of sorrow and distress. Funeral ceremonies and disposal of the body are also complex and varied, the main purpose being to ensure the safe return of the spirit to its totemic spirit home.

There were different ways of disposing of the dead. This could include burial in the ground or in a tree, a cave or rock shelter, or the body could be placed on a free-standing platform.

Funeral ceremonies were usually long and complex and could continue on long after the disposal of the corpse.

In many communities there is the custom of refraining from using the name of the deceased and to cover over any image of the dead person.

Ownership of land

Australia's first people own the land in a spiritual sense and this ownership is connected to religion. The events of the Dreamtime tell which group of people own which areas of land.

With ownership of land comes ritual responsibilities. Ritual owners have to ensure that ceremonies or rituals are performed at the proper times and proper place and that the ceremony is performed correctly. Because a lot of people are brought together for a ceremony a lot of organisation has to be done.

Ceremonial preparations can take days. The dance ground must be prepared, ritual paraphernalia made, bodies have to be painted. And because so many people are involved it is always important to hold ceremonies when there is plenty of food available in the bush.

Ownership of land is inherited from the father. It is also possible to inherit certain responsibilities for the mother's family land and ceremonies. So, while an Aboriginal person can be an owner of the land, he or she can also be a manager of the land and its ceremonies.

In the religion, the roles of owners and managers have to make sure that the spirit forces in the land are respected, that the spirit forces continue to use their powers for the good of all living things, that the religion is practised properly and that the laws laid down in the Dreamtime are obeyed.

Law

The laws that were laid down in the Dreamtime are known today as customary laws. Laws came from the Dreamtime when the Ancestral Beings formed the land, created all living things and established codes of behaviour and punishments.

In 1788 the British believed that Aboriginal Australians had no system of government or law. Gradually the Australian law courts accepted that Aboriginal people did have their own laws and a system for enforcing these laws.

Law courts today take into account customary law in deciding cases involving Indigenous people. Generally, the cases are those where an offence has been committed under traditional law.

Breaches of the law were usually announced loudly in the presence of others when it is safe. Those with complaints may wait till night-time when families are settled around the campfire. The person with a complaint would seek the support of senior men or women within the group. It was up to these law people to agree that an offence had been committed, to identify the offender and decide on suitable punishment.

Today Aboriginal and Torres Strait Islanders are subject to two separate legal systems. As well as customary law there is the Australian legal system which was inherited from the British.

Aboriginal legal services have been established throughout Australia the first one having been set up in Sydney, New South Wales in 1973.

Chapter 3

The Art of Australia's First People

Art and religion

The traditional art of Australia's first people was integrated into ceremony. It was part of religion and its production was tied to ceremony.

A design on the ground, on a body, a sculpture, or images drawn on a rock were manifestations of the Dreamtime or an event associated with a Dreamtime ancestral being.

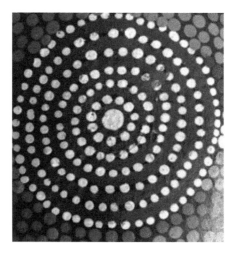

Concentric circles in desert art

Photograph by Marji Hill

A barramundi fish painted on a rock wall may be the Barramundi Ancestral Being while the geometric, abstract designs on a bark painting would tell the story of a Dreamtime saga. The 'U' shape and concentric circles of a desert ground painting would tell a Dreamtime story of one of the ancient heroes.

Traditional art was part of the expression of a major story or song cycle and part of ceremonial ritual. The aim of a ceremony was to evoke the power of the ancestral being and to encourage it to release again its creative powers.

A great creative saga was and is re-enacted in song, dance and art. Days can be spent in preparation for a ceremony making carvings, paintings, sand sculptures and other ritual items.

Not only does traditional art tell the stories of the Dreamtime but it provides a connection between human beings and the supernatural powers and linking them to particular sites in the landscape.

Another way of looking at some Aboriginal art is to look at it as a map of the countryside for all the parts of the relevant countryside are to be found in the artistic designs.

The creation of art was made in the context of religious ritual. The act of making it put its creators into communication with ancestral beings enabling them to tap into ancestral power. The artist in the process of creating reactivates the spiritual powers and brings them into direct relationship enabling the power to be tapped.

But to do this the artist can only ever paint or carve those designs and images that are relevant to him or her in a spiritual sense. There has to be a special totemic connection between the artist, the ancestral being and the art work being made.

Rock art

In the rock shelter known as Madjedbebe (formerly Malakunanja II) in the Northern Territory archaeologists suggest the cave was probably in use around 65 000 years ago.

This implies that Australian Aboriginal artists must have been making art in caves about 20000 years earlier than those who began painting in Europe.

Rock art

While painting on rock ended about 2000 years ago in Europe, the tradition of rock painting in Australia has continued to the present day, particularly at religious art sites in Arnhem Land in the Northern Territory, and the Kimberley in Western Australia.

As well as rock paintings the first Australians made rock engravings.

There are a number of rock engravings in Tasmania. At Mount Cameron West the motifs engraved into the rock are abstract and geometric with circles, crosses, rows of holes, animal tracks and trellis-like designs.

Other rock engravings are located at Devon Downs on the Murray River in South Australia, in the Northern Territory and in northern Queensland.

About 24,000 years ago early miners dug flint to make tools in Koonalda Cave which is situated in the Nullarbor Plain in South Australia. The miners went through a wide entrance into a sloping tunnel about 100 metres (328 feet) long which led to a room that is 76 metres (249.3 feet) below the surface.

At about 300 metres (984.2 feet) inside the cave there are wall markings that were deliberately made featuring a series of spaghetti like finger markings.

Rock art in the Kimberley, northwest of Western Australia, is well known for its Bradshaw figures and the Wandjina spirit figures.

The Bradshaw figures are like the Mimi (stick figures) found in Arnhem Land. This style of art was replaced by the Wandjinas.

Wandjinas are huge spirit beings, almost human in form, with large headdresses. The Wandjinas are believed to be the clouds which form before the rains begin and they are responsible for bringing the rains.

Wandjinas are very powerful spirit beings; they are so powerful that people today still take great care when approaching a Wandjina site. They call out to the spirit to let it know that they are coming and to assure the Wandjina that they will do no harm to its paintings.

Thousands of rock shelters containing paintings and engravings are located near Laura on Cape York Peninsula in North Queensland. The key spirit figures of this art work are the Quinkins which are usually painted in one colour, particularly red.

Quicken spirits are everywhere not only as images on the rock but they are living in the cracks of rocks. They come out to frighten people and to punish people if they have been offended.

The third major rock art site in Australia is in the Arnhem Land escarpment which are characterised by the Mimi stick like figures and the more recent X-ray paintings (see below).

Many rock art sites in Arnhem Land are sacred and cannot be visited by uninitiated people. However, there are some that can be visited like Obiri Rock (Ubir) in Kakadu National Park.

Mimi rock art shows images of frail people that are stick like in shape, but mystery surrounds these Mimi spirit figures. In caves and rock shelters around Oenpelli in Arnhem Land there are whole series of Mimi spirit paintings. Mimi are dancing, fighting, hunting and carrying the dead.

X-ray paintings are a more recent art than the Mimi as they overlay the earlier art. The distinctive feature is that the artists make images of totemic beings - animals, birds, reptiles and fish - and show their internal organs.

Modern Arnhem Land painting on slate

Photograph by Marji Hill

Bark paintings

Because bark paintings do not last for centuries like rock art it is hard to know when the people of Arnhem Land started making bark paintings. Bark paintings have been important in religious ceremonies in Arnhem Land.

Early white explorers found paintings on pieces of bark in many parts of Australia from Tasmania to Arnhem Land.

When missionaries, visiting scientists and government officers began collecting bark paintings Aboriginal Australians began to realise that their paintings and other art objects had an economic value in the western world.

Western Arnhem Land painters tend to set their figures against a background colour like red ochre, or white, yellow or black. The highly decorated figures and images may be divided into sections but do not fill the whole board. It is possible to identify the particular clan an artist belongs to from the cross-hatching designs he or she uses.

In eastern Arnhem Land, the style tends to be more abstract and geometric. Yolngu painters, for instance, lay out a basic pattern on a bark surface in yellow on a red ochre background. Then using a long brush made from human hair they paint intricate patterns of cross hatched lines.

In Central Arnhem Land the style tends to be a combination of both western and eastern Arnhem Land styles.

Relics of a past culture

At the turn of the nineteenth century there was considerable interest in Australian Aboriginal art and culture because it was the European view of the time that Australian Aboriginal people were a dying race and so too was its art and culture. Its art was regarded as art from a "primitive" society and therefore not true art.

Australian museums were building their collections. There was strong interest from other countries as well.

Spears, clubs, shields, fishing nets were collected at Port Jackson in Sydney and were sent back to England as souvenirs of the "Australian natives". Naval expeditions collected and recorded information about Aboriginal people. European museums were interested in ethnographic information and artefacts were collected and sold to overseas museums.

Aboriginal art of the time was something for museums and it was classified as artefacts and relics of a dying culture.

But while the European world was busy collecting remnants of this past culture Australia's first people started to accommodate the dramatic changes that had taken place in their culture. Aboriginal artists began adapting to the new and changed set of circumstances.

A new emerging art

William Barak (1824-1903) was an artist and a leader of the Woiwurrong people whose country lay in and around Melbourne in Victoria. William was a boy when the British took over his lands and he was educated in an Anglican mission. However, he held on to his traditional religious knowledge and using a European brush he painted water colours on cardboard recording the customs and life of his people.

Another Victorian, Tommy McRae (c.1820s-1901) came from the upper Murray Valley region. He drew lively pictures in ink which recalled much of his life's experience. His images show Aboriginal people hunting and performing ceremonial dances.

McRae's drawings showed a changing world. In one drawing he has a European house; in another he has a Chinese violin player and a drummer beating out the music for a dance.

The idea of Aboriginal people being artists emerged more forcefully in the late 1930s with the success of Albert Namatjira (1902-1959) as a water colourist. He painted central Australian landscapes and had his first solo exhibition in Melbourne in 1938.

Namatjira was an Aranda man from Hermannsburg in Central Australia. Traditional art of the region was in the form of ground paintings, body art and visual art involving wood and stone. It was ceremonial art with dance, music and song and it belonged to the realm of initiated men.

Painting in the style of Albert Namatjira by Gabriel Namatjira

Photograph by Marji Hill

Namatjira was innovative and he learnt to paint the landscape under the mentorship of Rex Battarbee. He perfected the water colour technique and he saw how painting in the European way provided a fresh opportunity.

The 1950s and 1960s saw the art of Aboriginal Australia making an impact on the general Australian art world.

When art galleries and private collectors were beginning to look for works of art by Aboriginal artists access to their work was being made easier by the encouragement of the missionaries. The stage was finally being set for the emergence of Aboriginal art into the world of contemporary art.

Renaissance of Aboriginal art

The renaissance of Aboriginal art took place from the mid 1970s when it emerged as an outstanding contemporary fine art tradition just as genuine as the art that was made prior to European contact.

While Aboriginal art traditionally was motivated by religious and spiritual reasons there came into being a shift in that motivation. Art making now enabled artists to have an economic base in a capitalist world. Contemporary Aboriginal artists had a means of producing income.

The early 1970s saw the evolution of dot painting from the traditional ground paintings.

In 1971 a European art teacher, Geoffrey Bardon, at Papanya wanted a mural painted onto a wall of the school building.

He set his students to work on painting the mural.

Then the senior men took over because they were concerned that the boys were attempting to paint desert stories which did not belong to them. First, they had to agree that the designs put on the wall could be viewed by everyone - men, women and children.

Finally, Old Tom Onion Tjapangati, gave permission for them to paint the Honey Ant Dreaming which he owned.

This unleashed a fervent artistic activity with the men painting their designs on anything and everything.

This activity was a watershed in the history of Australian Aboriginal art.

Painting on board and then canvas using acrylic paints became the new trend and it was not long before the central Australian artists started selling their works of art.

While initially sales were only a few dollars for a painting by the late 1980s paintings were commanding thousands of dollars.

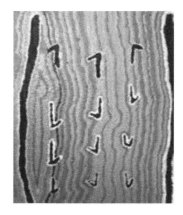

Desert painting in acrylic on canvas by Lady Nungarrayi Robertson

Photograph by Marji Hill

Desert art

Among the many forms of art in the desert art were the ephemeral drawings made in sand which were either quickly rubbed out or were left to be blown away by the wind.

There were rock engravings and cave paintings.

On the surface to a European viewer desert art looks abstract and geometrical. It is characterised by its spirals, lines, circles and points.

But to the Aboriginal desert eye the designs represent the landscape as if seen by a bird flying overhead. To a bird a campsite looks circular, as does a well, a rock or a hill. A horseshoe design can represent a person sitting or it could represent a windbreak.

Desert designs made by the men of the central desert are the Dreaming tracks on which the great ancestral beings travelled.

The Dreaming tracks connect the story places which are important religious sites in the men's countries.

All desert artists use the same symbols in their art works and once you know the symbols and what they mean it is possible to understand the designs.

The symbols may have different layers of meaning and mean different things depending on how they are placed in relation to other symbols used in the paintings.

The art movement that started in Papunya eventually spread to Yuendumu and many other communities in Central Australia. Communities like Balgo, Fitzroy Crossing in Western Australia developed their own distinctive art movements.

What started as a ceremonial and religious art was transformed into a secular art. Designs put onto canvas were such that they could be viewed by the uninitiated.

Desert art became something that could be successfully marketed in the western world and western context. Art works became investment items and as such dot painting became big industry.

Art and land ownership

Aboriginal art that was originally motivated by religious reasons was used in some circumstances to make political statements in a changing world that became dominated by Western culture.

In 1963 the Yirrkala people of North East Arnhem Land presented their bark petition to the Australian Parliament - the House of Representatives in Canberra. Using clan designs the petition shows all the areas of country that were under threat from mining. These designs represented the Yirrkala title to land.

In 1976 the Australian Government passed a new law which made it possible for Aboriginal people in the Northern Territory to claim land that they could prove they traditionally owned. According to the law the land had to be owned by the Government (Crown Land) and not in use. To prove that they were the real traditional owners they had to use their religious knowledge of sites and Dreaming tracks.

In 1978 the Anmatyerre and the Alyawarra people used their ancient stories and designs to prove that they were the traditional owners of an area called Utopia, northeast of Alice Springs.

The paintings made by the Spinifex People (Anangu Tjuta Pila Nguru) of the Great Victoria Desert are a fine example of art being used for political purposes and proving title to land.

In 1998 the Premier of Western Australia announced that the Spinifex People were the traditional owners they claimed. This was 55,000 kilometres of sandhill, mulga plain and spinifex bush located between the Nullarbor Plain and the Warburton Ranges.

These paintings claiming title to land have political themes relevant to the modern world. At the same time, they are based on the fundamental principles of traditional religion.

Art became a means of proving title to land. It was used as a title deed. A title deed in the European sense is a legal document showing ownership of property so Australian Aboriginal art is like a title deed. The story of particular tracts of land are documented in the paintings.

This knowledge that has been passed through the generations using art and stories is now recognised by the Australian legal system as part of the proof of traditional ownership of land.

Contemporary art

Urban Aboriginal artists see themselves in the mainstream of Australian art. Their themes are commonly to do with social comment and political expression.

Among the earliest artists to gain formal art qualifications was Trevor Nickolls when in 1970 he got a Diploma in Fine Art from the South Australian School of Art. His art sets out to state his own Aboriginality and his links to the Dreamtime. At the same time, he tells of his urban upbringing and his links to city life.

The Boomalli Aboriginal Artists Cooperative in Sydney which offered its members workspace and opportunities to exhibit their work held its first exhibition in 1987. Its early members were Avril Quail, Bronwyn Bancroft, Euphemia Bostock, Brenda Croft, Fiona Foley, Raymond Meeks and Jeffrey Samuels.

The Cooperative was influential in helping artists develop and promote their work and these early members all went on to establish successful careers as Australian contemporary artists.

Lin Onus (1948-1996) was one of the outstanding artists of his generation. His paintings combine a photographic approach to the landscape with an infusion of floating Aboriginal symbols. Having grown up in a politically active household, Lin Onus played an active role in Aboriginal affairs.

Onus had many successful exhibitions and won a number of prestigious art awards. In 1994 his painting "Barmah Forest" won both the main award and the People's Choice Award at the First National Aboriginal and Torres Strait Islander Heritage Arts Award in Canberra.

This Telstra National Aboriginal and Torres Strait Islander Art Award recognises the contribution of Aboriginal and Torres Strait Islander artists working in both traditional and contemporary media, and the quality and diversity of art produced in Australia.

It is the longest running Aboriginal art award and it still runs today. The 2020 award was won by Ngarralja Tommy May for his etching on metal and enamel paint.

Jimmy Pike, a Walmajarri man, from the Great Sandy Desert in Western Australia, developed a reputation in 1980 as an artist while being in prison in Fremantle. His art was marketed through a company called Desert Designs and he became an internationally renowned artist with exhibitions in Australia and overseas.

These artists have based their art on their Aboriginality while expressing their personal experiences, observations and dreams in their own style using contemporary artistic materials.

If you browse through the lists of contemporary artists in the Creative Spirits website you will see that contemporary Aboriginal artists - visual artists, photographers and writers - are many and varied. There are just too many to incorporate here. It is so evident that Aboriginal Australian art has gained a prominence with thousands of Aboriginal artists producing innovative works of art and making art today.

The art of the first people in Australia has witnessed new motivations in its making. It has incorporated Western paints and materials; it has experimented with a wider palette using many different colours, fresh imagery such as boats, guns, horses; and, there has been innovation in design.

Aboriginal art represents the continuity of a culture - an art tradition that started 65,000 years ago and has continued to this present day.

While art in many parts of eastern and southern Australia came close to being destroyed, art overall throughout Australia has adapted, been innovative, and been modified in response to the Western presence in this country.

The art of the desert, the art of the north, south, east and west, together with the art of the urban areas demonstrates just how much strength and vitality Aboriginal cultures have had in the face of their almost tragic cultural dispossession.

Far from being a product of a bygone era Australian Aboriginal art is like a living organism; it evolves, adapts, and changes. It has demonstrated how Aboriginal culture in its need to survive has been resilient and how Aboriginal Australians are stepping forth in independence and reconciliation and paving the way for a new and fresh future.

Chapter 4

Living with the Land

Aboriginal people who lived close to waterways and the ocean had access to plentiful food resources. Food was nutritious and there was plenty of protein either from the land or sea. There was a rich variety of vegetable foods. The daily task of hunting and gathering food would only take a few hours of "labour" each day.

So daily life for the first people prior to the British invasion in 1788 could easily be described as affluent.

In Victoria at Lake Condah, the Gunditjmara people established an extensive farming system to trap eels. This farming method included smoking techniques to preserve the eels. There was an eel industry and eels were traded with others as far away as South Australia and New South Wales. In return for the eels the Gunditjmara got quartz and flint to make stone knives and other stone implements.

It was easy for the Gunditjmara to obtain their regular food supply which included not only eel but possum and kangaroo.

Life could be described as sedentary. A growing body of evidence points to the fact that the Gunditjmara built stone villages.

For a long time there has been the common misconception that Aboriginal people were "nomadic", that they wandered aimlessly, desperately searching for food and water - a constant struggle for survival.

But Aboriginal people wanted to remain close to their own lands. The reason was twofold: to be close to the land because of the special spiritual links and ties, and because of their knowledge of the country which guaranteed their ability to survive.

Land owning group

The major land-owning group in Australia is commonly called a "tribe". However, this term is not accurate as it does not reflect the Australian system of social organisation. A tribe is a form of political organisation that has never existed in Australia. Nonetheless, the word "tribe" has crept into popular usage.

The basic social unit was and still is the family. Small family groups would come together and form a "band". A band might be made up of 25 to 50 people from one or more families.

Families would live and hunt together. These family groupings are quite different to a "clan".

A clan is a group of people who are all descended from a common ancestor so a band or group of families could be made up of several clans. That common ancestor could be Kangaroo, Cockatoo or Echidna. People cannot marry members of the same clan.

In a band you might find that an Echidna person is married to a Kangaroo or a Magpie is married to a Koala. A band is therefore a residential group and a clan a descent group descending from a common ancestor.

Members of a clan share the ritual responsibility of caring for the land that they own. A clan comes together for ritual and ceremonial purposes, to arrange marriages, to settle interclan disputes and to share seasonably abundant resources. It is the clan that is the major political unit in Australian Aboriginal society.

Kinship

All over the world people organise themselves in different ways according to relationships with one another. Everyone has a number of relatives. Kinship ties define the relationship a person has to their relatives.

In Australian Aboriginal cultures a person's circle of relatives plays an important part in social life. Aboriginal people need to know how those around them are related so that they know how to behave appropriately towards a person.

This strength of family ties and awareness of family obligations is a distinguishing characteristic of Aboriginal and Torres Strait Island people not only in the past but today as well.

Their system of kinship may seem complex but Aboriginal children learn these relationships while growing up in the family unit.

They learn the appropriate way to address a relative, how they should behave to that person and what their responsibilities are to certain relatives.

Some important relatives, for instance, are mother's sister. This person is called "mother". A father's father is called "father". "Mother's brother" plays an important role for boys because they are usually responsible for the boy's initiation.

Kinship laws require that marriage takes place outside their own line of descent. This means that a Kangaroo person cannot marry another Kangaroo but a Kangaroo could marry a Magpie.

Living off the land

Australia's first people then and now are hunter-gatherers. They find their food from their land.

Traditionally men fished and hunted for larger game like kangaroos or dugong while women gathered plants and small animals.

Men made the tools: knives, scrapers, axe-heads, spears, boomerangs, clubs - tools that were designed for hunting.

Men would hunt the animals, spear the fish, catch a turtle or dugong, a goanna or emu. They recognised the marks left on the ground by the different animals. They could tell the recency of the marks and where to find their prey. Usually hunters worked as a team and shared the game they caught.

The men used spears to catch large animals or to catch large sea creatures. There were several kinds of spears with different designs. A multi-pronged spear would be used for fishing.

Aboriginal club

Photograph by Marji Hill

To help a spear travel at a greater speed and with greater force Aboriginal men invented a wooden spear throwing device. This was called a woomera.

Fire, traps and ambush were other methods used for hunting. Today men might use guns.

Women went out in groups. They gathered the food and hunted for small animals all of which provided the staple diet.

They would dig up root plants, gather bulbs, collect seed, pick fruit and catch any small animals or reptiles like bandicoots or lizards, or gather shellfish if living by the sea.

Women had their own tool sets which they used to collect food. Their main tool was the digging stick which they used to dig small animals and roots out of the ground.

When the women found the food, they held it in a wooden dish. They carried dilly bags to hold small implements and they used grinding stones to prepare vegetable food.

Depending on the climate and the environment there was usually a wide choice of food.

Hunters and gatherers in Australia developed many sophisticated ways to collect food.

As has already been mentioned, at Lake Condah in Western Victoria extensive drainage channels were built to catch eels. Traps were placed across the channels to catch the eels as they were carried down in the flowing water. The channels were blocked at their mouths to stop the flow of water once the traps held as many eels as were needed.

Traps for catching ducks were identified on the Darling River at Brewarrina in New South Wales. The bird nets were 90 metres long and several metres deep. They stretched across the river enabling up to 100 ducks to be netted at once.

The Kombumerri people of the Gold Coast in Southeast Queensland used dolphins to force fish close into the shore. This meant large quantities of fish could be speared or scooped up in butterfly shaped nets.

In contrast to people living in desert areas, Yugambeh families in Southeast Queensland, had access to plenty of food. In the space of an hour, they could collect enough food to last each family for a day.

Kombumerri people living in the Gold Coast region trapped possums, wallabies, kangaroos and other animals that grazed in the open forests.

Not all plant foods were readily available for eating. Because some plants were poisonous, they had to be treated. Other foods had to be mashed and leached in water before they could be cooked or eaten.

Cycad nuts, which contained a poisonous substance but were a good source of energy, had to undergo special preparation before eating.

The nuts had to be ground and placed in a bag in water for a while. The pulp was squeezed, made into cakes and then baked in the ashes of a fire.

This hunter-gatherer lifestyle provided for a balanced diet and demanded less labour than the European style of agriculture. It assured the continued availability of food.

Not only was there time for hunting and gathering time was available to pursue religious and creative activities.

Fire

Fire was an important tool for farming in Aboriginal Australia. It has been used as a tool by Aboriginal people for thousands and thousands of years.

In 1969 prehistorian, Rhys Jones, propounded the concept of "fire-stick farming" which meant fire was used as a tool and as a means of land management.

Pascoe (2014) referred to the early observers of Aboriginal Australia who noted a "mosaic pattern of low-level burns" and frequent low scale burning.

In pre-colonial times Aboriginal Australians practised controlled burning to clear the land. This was a means of weed control and a method for clearing undergrowth.

Controlled burns stimulated the regeneration of fresh grass and saplings, helped the regrowth of plants, and ensured a plentiful supply of food. Overall fire was used to increase the productivity of the environment.

Firestick farming was a method for coaxing wildlife to come and graze on the fresh grass which in turn facilitated hunting. When the animals were eating the fresh grass Aboriginal hunters could more easily catch and kill their prey.

Fire was used, not only for the easier spearing of game, it was also used to clear undergrowth so that there would be fresh regrowth of plants.

Wiradjuri people used fire to open up forest areas. Fire stimulated the growth of young trees. Fresh grass grew. This attracted animals to graze which ensured a plentiful food supply for the Wiradjuri.

Fire in the Aboriginal Australian world was an integral part of life. Not only was fire used to manage the land, but it was also a tool for preparing and shaping wooden implements.

Fire was essential for cooking; and, it was used to boil and dye grasses that are woven into bags and baskets.

People gathered around hearth fires as they repaired tools, wove baskets, talked, taught children or prepared food for a meal.

In ceremonies, fire provided the smoke to purify those taking part and to drive away spirits of the dead.

It was made by striking a hard rock surface to produce a spark or by using friction. If two dry wooden surfaces were rubbed together at high speed it was possible to produce enough heat to cause a flame.

One friction technique was to make a shallow hole in a piece of wood and then fill it with sawdust. The sharpened end of another piece of wood was then pushed down into the hole and spun quickly backwards and forwards.

The friction eventually caused the sawdust to glow. The burning sawdust was then poured into a nest of dried grass and blown on until the grass burst into flame.

Boomerang

A boomerang is type of throwing stick. Aboriginal people were the first to understand the principles of aerodynamics with the creation of the boomerang with one arm angled at about 120 degrees to the other.

Properly thrown a boomerang should return. The top and bottom sides of each arm are carved so that when the boomerang is thrown with a spin, the air flowing over the surface will force the stick into a rising curve outwards and then on a descending curve inwards.

Boomerangs were not used all over Australia. For instance they were not in Tasmania, Cape York, parts of Arnhem Land, the Kimberley coast or parts of South Australia.

There are different types of boomerangs. Some lighter ones are used to frighten nesting birds. They whirr over the tops of trees frightening the birds so that the birds fly into the nets of hunters.

Other larger, heavier boomerangs are used to injure large game like kangaroos.

Boomerangs are also used for ceremonial purposes. If clapped together they become a musical instrument to accompany ceremonial dancers.

Larger and heavy boomerangs have been used in fighting and others have been used as tools - for cutting, digging, making fire. Boomerangs have also been used as items of trade and exchange.

Watercraft

Canoes were used to travel over water - lagoons, rivers and ocean. Makeshift rafts were made to cross rivers, or a simple canoe was the bark canoe. This was made from a single sheet of thick bark. The ends were pointed and the bark moulded into shape over a smoky fire to form a boat.

A second type of canoe was made from large cylindrical sheets of bark which were turned inside-out and bound at the ends with rope made of fibre. Stretchers and pliant branches were put across the canoe which acted as ribs.

Canoe trees can still be seen today within the Murray-Darling Basin. These trees have scars resulting from the removal of a large slab of bark from which a canoe was made.

Dugout canoes, crafted from tree trunks, were used in north Australia and in the Torres Strait seafarers designed boats with sails, outriggers and paddles.

Didjeridu

The didjeridu (or didgeridoo) is a musical instrument that produces a rhythmical droning sound. They are made from logs hollowed out by fire or termites and then cleaned out. Bamboo can also be used.

A didjeridu varies in length from 100 (39.3 inches) to 160 centimetres (63 inches). It is narrower at one end for the mouthpiece.

Didjeridus designed for the tourist market

Photograph by Marji Hill

The instrument is played by filling the cheeks with breath and keeping up a continual flow of air into the hollow tube. This is achieved by sucking air into the cheeks through the nose.

The sound produced varies according to the length of the instrument.

Traditionally the didjeridu was used in ceremonial performances and would be decorated with clan designs. It originated from northern Australia and could be found from the Gulf of Carpentaria to Derby in Western Australia.

Nowadays, the didjeridu is an instrument that is being played and taught all around the world and it has been embraced by Aboriginal people throughout Australia. It has become synonymous with Aboriginal Australia just like the boomerang.

Housing

Traditional housing was built from trees, shrubs, shell and stone. Sometimes a house would be a simple shelter designed for a short, overnight stay. At the other end of the spectrum there were permanent houses built of stone.

Torres Strait Islanders had a form of permanent housing. A dome-shaped style of house with a round floor and a central pole was used. The roof and walls were made of bamboo ribs, bent and tied into a beehive shape, and then thatched with tightly packed grass that kept out the rain and the wind. They were decorated with large shells.

On the mainland some housing was designed for hot dry areas. People built small, curved shelters to protect them from the wind and the sun. In the desert Aboriginal people built light windbreaks or shades made from the branches of trees and sticks.

In the northern Australia where heavy monsoonal rains fall in summer, houses were built on stumps above the ground. These houses had bark roofs and walls to keep out the rain. They were high enough off the ground for a smoky fire to be built underneath to drive away the mosquitoes.

On the west coast of Tasmania housing was conical. They were thatched with grass and were large enough to hold about thirty people and were designed to keep out the cold. Up to seventeen houses were built in a village.

Housing in communities today is not much different to housing found in other parts of Australia. The only difference is that people might prefer to live under a house if it is high enough off the ground or outside the house around a fire.

In cities and towns Aboriginal people live in houses with all the modern conveniences just like their non-Indigenous neighbours.

Trade and exchange

Aboriginal people had an elaborate system of trade throughout the continent. Trade routes were established that crisscrossed the countryside from Cape York in north Queensland down to the South Australian coast, northwest to the Kimberley and the Daly River and south again to Perth.

These trade routes would cross the country owned by other people. Provided people remained on the identified trade routes and did not offend those whose country they were passing through along the way, they were safe to travel.

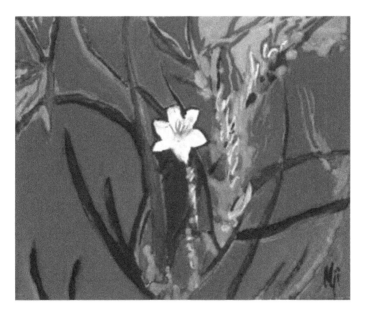

Pituri   Art work by Marji Hill

People travelled long distances to trade and to get goods that they wanted. One trader might spread out in front of him a set of beautifully carved and decorated boomerangs. Another might offer a bag of dried pituri.

Pituri is a native tobacco plant which has a high nicotine content. When chewed pituri leaves produce a narcotic effect.

Large quantities of pituri used to be traded as far north around the Gulf of Carpentaria and to the south around Port Augusta in South Australia. The most highly prized variety of pituri came from Southwest Queensland.

People in southern Australia were able to get carved pearl shells from the northwest coast or bags of dried pituri.

Ceremonies were taught to people as far away in the south and west of Australia.

Other goods that were traded included shell, wood, gum and a variety of tools, ornaments and sacred objects. Different types of stone were traded.

Axe heads from a quarry at Mount William in Victoria found their way to South Australia and New South Wales. Other axe heads from Queensland quarries travelled along the river systems to Lake Eyre and Central Australia.

Rare types of top-quality red ochres were available thousands of kilometres away from where they were sourced.

Preserved eel from Lake Condah in Victoria was traded as far away as South Australia and New South Wales.

Major meetings between groups took place with people coming together to perform ceremonies, arrange marriages, and to settle disputes. These gatherings offered the opportunity to trade and to exchange gifts.

Chapter 5

The Unknown Continent

Prior to 1788, when the British invaded the east coast of Australia, there were a number of visitors to what was regarded as that strange and unknown continent. When the first visitors came is not known.

But there has long been contact with the people of Papua New Guinea for many thousands of years. When the sea levels were low the two countries - Papua New Guinea and Australia - were connected by land. This was during the Ice Ages. The people of Papua New Guinea, and those of the Torres Strait and Cape York Peninsula intermarried and exchanged cultural values and technology.

The Chinese admiral Cheng Ho sailed into regions bordering the Indian Ocean, including East Africa, India, Java and Sumatra. Who knows he may even have travelled into Australian waters between 1405 and 1432 on his great voyages of discovery.

Macassans

For a period of several hundred years to just after the conclusion of the nineteenth century at least 1000 Macassans from the Indonesian island of Sulewesi visited northern Australia. They were fishermen and they fished for the sea slug called trepang. This was a prized delicacy in Chinese cuisine.

Each year the Macassans would come. They would stay in northern Australia for approximately five months before heading back in April of each year when the winds changed to the southeast.

Macassans came by sea to northern Australia.

Artwork by Marji Hill

Macassans set up settlements on sheltered beaches along the coast of Arnhem Land not far from the shallow waters where the trepang was collected. They set up processing plants for the trepang also known as *beche-de-mer*.

Rows of stone fireplaces were built which supported the cauldrons in which the trepang was boiled. The second stage of the processing involved burying the trepang in the sand. It was smoked and then packed ready to be taken back to Macassar and the markets in Asia.

A lively trade went on between the Macassans and the local Aboriginal people. The Yolngu of northeast Arnhem Land exchanged turtle shell, pearl shell and cypress timber for knives, axes and tobacco. Macassan words crept into the local language and the dugout canoe and Macassan pipe were introduced.

Some Aboriginal families today have Macassan ancestors and relations and there are those who even travelled back to Macassar.

The remains of Macassan camps can be seen along the northern coast and are usually marked by tamarind trees which grew from seeds left behind by the Macassan visitors.

In 1907 the Australian government put an end to these visits by the Macassans because they became a threat to the pearling industry.

The Portuguese and Spanish

In the sixteenth and seventeenth centuries Portuguese and Spanish navigators explored the waters near Australia. In 1605 the Spanish navigator, Pedro Fernandes de Queirós claimed Vanuatu thinking it was the great southern land, and Luis Vaez de Torres in 1606 sailed through the waters that now bear his name - the Torres Strait.

The Dutch

In that same year 1606, the Dutch explored the waters around the northern, western and southern coasts. There were some unfriendly encounters with Aboriginal people which dissuaded them from exploring inland. In 1697 Willem de Vlamingh made an attempt at exploration but he also withdrew.

The French

The inspiration of Napoleon Bonaparte as Emperor of the French carried the French to far corners of the globe.

Between 1771 and 1828 the French sent eight expeditions to Australia to expand their knowledge of the little- known world of Australia and the Pacific. Many places in Australia were named after the French explorers: La Perouse, D'Entrecasteaux Channel, Freycinet, to name just a few.

Captain Nicolas Baudin commanding *Le Geographe* and *La Naturaliste* arrived in Western Australia in 1801. In February

1803 Baudin and his men established contact with the Nyungar people at King George Sound.

The age-old rivalry between England and France flared as soon as the French flag was seen in Australian waters. Suspicious that France might claim and colonise that half of the continent not covered by Cook's proclamation in 1770 led the British to establish garrisons in northern and southern Australia in the 1820s.

The English

On 19 April 1770 Captain James Cook reached the east coast of Australia. Cook was instructed to take possession of the eastern half of the continent for the British crown.

At Possession Island, off Cape York Peninsula in North Queensland, he took possession of the whole of the eastern coast in the name of King George III.

Cook declared that Australia was *terra nullius* meaning that Australia was a land without people and that it was unoccupied and unowned. Therefore, the belief of the time was that the English could justify claiming the country as theirs.

1788

The arrival of the First Fleet from England in 1788 changed the course of history for Aboriginal people of Australia forever. For the next two hundred years a tragic and catastrophic history unfolded which for Aboriginal people was marked by constant warfare with their British invaders.

The first wars of resistance wars began in Sydney in the 1790s and it was the people known as the Eora who were the first of the Aboriginal nations to defend their land.

On 10 December 1790 an Aboriginal guerrilla leader got a notation in Governor Arthur Phillip's dispatches. This was

Pemulwuy and for the next 12 years he led the resistance against the New South Wales Corp in the Sydney region.

Pemulwuy

Pemulwuy was an Eora man who led the battle against the British who occupied their lands in the late 1700s.

Pemulwuy's name was linked to the killing of Governor Phillip's gamekeeper called McIntyre.

Artist's impression of Pemulwuy by Marji Hill

He would attack British settlers and their properties so soldiers were sent out to arrest him but they did not succeed.

In 1795 it was thought that Pemulwuy had been killed by a bushranger named Black Caesar. Pemulwuy was badly wounded but he survived, and he continued his fierce attacks against the British invaders.

Eventually in a battle at Parramatta he was wounded and captured, but he escaped death and was once again leading the attacks.

In 1801 Governor Philip Gidley King tried to turn the Eora people in Parramatta, Georges River and Prospect Hill against Pemulwuy. He told them that friendly relations would be restored when Pemulwuy's head was brought into the settlement.

In 1802 Pemulwuy was shot by two settlers and his head cut off. The head was preserved in spirits and sent to England for research.

Resistance

Not only the Eora, but the neighbouring Dharuk people fought for their lands.

Another resistance fighter emerged in the Hawkesbury River area. This was Musquito. He led many of the attacks on settlers and their property along the New South Wales Central coast.

After being captured and imprisoned on Norfolk Island he was in 1813 sent to Tasmania (in those days called Van Dieman's Land). There he volunteered to track down bushrangers and was promised his freedom if successful. The promise, however, was never kept.

In about 1819 Musquito joined the Tasmanian Oyster Bay people who ran a resistance campaign against the British.

In 1824 a reward was offered for his capture. He was tracked down and shot and eventually hung for murder.

Dispossession and almost genocide characterised the occupation of Aboriginal country for the next one hundred years. As white settlement spread throughout the continent paramilitary forces such as the Native Mounted Police were set up to combat the resistance.

Wars of resistance against the British

Artwork by Marji Hill

Resistance moved over the Great Dividing Range with the crossing of the Blue Mountains in 1813. Following the example of the Eora in Sydney the Wiradjuri challenged the British presence for many long and terrible months. One of their resistance fighters, Windradyne, emerged as a leader of his people.

Windradyne led raids throughout 1823 and he and his warriors attacked outlying stations. The stubborn resistance of the Wiradjuri caused the then Governor Thomas Brisbane to declare martial law in the Bathurst district in 1824.

Battles turned into massacres and one third of the Wiradjuri population in the area was killed. Small groups of Wiradjuri began to surrender.

Windradyne and about 400 of his people trekked 200 kilometres from the Bathurst district to Parramatta for a peace meeting with Governor Brisbane.

Five years later Windradyne died of a wound he received in a dispute with other Wiradjuri people.

By the late 1830s the British intruded into the lands of the Kamilaroi who were pushed from their water supplies and robbed of their game.

1838 saw the massacre of Aboriginal men, women and children at Myall Creek near the Gwyder River in northern New South Wales. By the end of the 1830s, the resistance wars stretched from northern New South Wales to western Victoria.

Resistance wars continued out from the east to all parts of the Australian continent. In Western Australia when hostilities broke out with the British, another resistance hero emerged. This was Yagan, who became a war leader in the tradition established by Pemulwuy.

Yagan's story is about the invasion of Nyungar lands in the west by the British and how Aboriginal people fiercely defended their rights and their lands.

In the Mt Isa region of North Queensland, the Kalkadoon wars culminated in 1884 with the clash of Battle Mountain.

In the 1890s another resistance leader, Jandamarra, defended Bunuba lands. He led the insurrection against the British invaders in the Kimberley region in the far north of Western Australia.

Aboriginal cultures of eastern Australia bore the full brunt of the British occupation of their lands and it was they who were the first to experience the dispossession of their cultures. What took place in eastern Australia was repeated throughout the continent. There was no discussion with Aboriginal people, no treaty, and tragedy continued to unfold.

Before the invasion by the British, Aborigines of Australia had defined territories and knew the boundaries of their traditional lands. They knew its physical features, its geography, animals, birds, fish and plants. They looked after their lands and ritually cared for their country with ceremony, songs, stories and art.

But with the invasion and the taking over of traditional lands for farming, Australian Aboriginal cultures were almost destroyed. They fought to defend their country from the north to the south and from the east to the west.

With so much devastation, killings and introduced diseases the Aboriginal population declined, and authorities believed that the race was dying out.

Protection policy

From the early 1800s Aboriginal people started moving to missions that were being established. In the missions they were taught European beliefs and the Christian religion. They also became a source of cheap labour.

When it seemed that Aboriginal people were going to die out the British decided "to protect" the surviving people.

Many had died as a result of violent conflict while others were forced to live on government rations and suffered malnutrition and disease. Because colonial governments (Australia did not have a Federal government until 1901) thought Aboriginal people were on their way to becoming extinct they introduced protectionist legislation. This protectionist legislation was designed to control and segregate Aboriginal people from mainstream white society - deciding where and how they should live.

Various denominations of missionaries set up mission stations in different parts of the continent. The plan was to protect Aboriginal people and train them in Christian ideals. Around ten missions were set up in New South Wales alone.

The Lutherans established a mission in the 1860s for the desert people of South Australia. This was Killalpaninna. Aboriginal people were encouraged to move there to get protection from the intrusion of Europeans on to their lands and to have sanctuary from the new and threatening world.

1869 saw the establishment of the Victorian Board for the Protection of Aborigines. Children could be removed to a reformatory or industrial school or removed from station families to be housed in dormitories. The other colonies followed suit with New South Wales (1883), Queensland (1897), Western Australia (1905) and South Australia (1911).

Laws designed to protect Aboriginal people meant government authorities, like a Chief Protector or Protection Board, were given extensive powers to control Aboriginal people. In some States and the Northern Territory these authorities became the legal guardians of Aborigines. Parents lost all rights to their children. These laws caused a further breakdown of traditional Aboriginal culture.

In 1883 when the Aborigines Protection Board in New South Wales had been set up to "care" for Aboriginal Australians it had the power to remove children from their parents and families. It was also illegal for people of mixed descent to live on Aboriginal reserves.

Activism

The Depression years of the 1920s and 1930s were very hard on Aboriginal people. Work was even more difficult for them than it was for other unemployed Australians.

An activist emerged who started fighting for Aboriginal rights. This was William Ferguson (1882-1950). His mother was a Wiradjuri woman and his father, a Scottish boundary rider.

Being a shearer, Ferguson moved around New South Wales during the war years (1939-1945) and he observed the poor and terrible conditions under which Aboriginal people lived.

Ferguson was active in the Australian Workers Union and he was a member of the Australian Labor Party.

Ferguson was very concerned about the Aborigines Protection Board and he looked for help from the Labor Party supporters and other Aboriginal people who shared his concern. He formed the Aborigines Progressive Association with the aim of getting full citizen rights for Aboriginal people. He wanted to see their representation in Parliament, and the abolition of the Aborigines Protection Board.

At the same time a Yorta Yorta man, William Cooper (c.1860-1941), was also fighting for Aboriginal rights.

By 1935 Cooper had helped establish the Australian Aborigines League. Cooper organised a petition seeking direct representation in parliament, enfranchisement and land rights and he decided to petition King George V.

Cooper joined forces with Jack Patten and William Ferguson from the Aborigines Progressive Association to organise a protest to shame white Australia.

1938 was the 150th anniversary of the British occupation of Australia so on 26 January of that year the activists declared it a Day of Mourning and Aboriginal Australians from all over New South Wales and Victoria came to join the protest meeting. More protest occurred in 1939 when over 150 Aboriginal people from Cummeragunja Mission in New South Wales packed up and walked away from the cruel treatment and exploitation by the management.

William Ferguson and William Cooper were resistance heroes who struggled for respect and recognition, and for equality and justice.

Assimilation policy (1937-1965)

In April 1937 a conference of Commonwealth and State authorities decided on an official policy for some Aboriginal people. This was the assimilation policy.

People of mixed descent were to be assimilated into white society. The implication of such a policy meant that Aboriginal people of mixed descent would lose their Aboriginal identity and culture and that over time Aborigines in this country would eventually disappear.

From the mid-nineteenth century, Australian colonial and state governments adopted 'protective' legislation and policies to control and segregate Aboriginal people from the white population, and from each other.

Government policies were enforced by white 'protectors' who administered the reserves and missions and had wide-ranging powers. In the name of 'protection,' governments directed where and how Aboriginal people should live.

Government policies of protection denied Aboriginal people their independence and their basic human rights.

From the late 1950s, both Indigenous and non-Indigenous activists campaigned for equal civil rights for Aboriginal Australians and fought for the repeal of laws which deprived Aborigines of civil liberties.

Various state laws made it impossible to be both an Australian citizen and an Aboriginal person. These were referred to as "dog collar acts" due to their restrictive nature especially in relation to Aboriginal people's association with their own families.

To escape the restrictions of these state laws anyone defined as an "Aborigine" had to seek an exemption. It was as if they were like a dog on a leash. If exempted authorities made unreasonable demands and that person was often no longer considered an "Aborigine" making it impossible to be an Aboriginal person and an Australian citizen at the same time.

In 1958, at a meeting in Adelaide, activists from all states formed the Federal Council for Aboriginal Advancement (FCAA). The first two goals of this new body were to repeal the legislation which discriminated against Aboriginal Australians and to amend the Commonwealth Constitution to give the Commonwealth Government power to legislate for Aboriginal people as with all other citizens.

While the population of Aborigines of full descent declined, the population of mixed descent increased. Governments decided that people of mixed descent should be brought into the Australian workforce so they didn't have to depend on government rations. They would be forced to take on the values of white Australia.

Laws were passed permitting governments to remove children of mixed descent from their families and place them with white families for whom they would work.

Children could be removed from a very early age. They were made to live in dormitories until the age of fourteen. Then they were sent off to work on missions, in settlements, or had to work for white families.

The policy of assimilation meant that in 1937 children of mixed descent had to be educated in the European system. If they were educated into adopting white values, they would take their place in white society.

By 1941 state government institutions and missions were given extra funding to remove even more children from their families. The reason was that they were "neglected" children. As the institutions became overcrowded more and more children were placed into white families.

Even the identities of these children were denied. The children were given new names and all effort went into ensuring that these children never saw their parents again.

Freedom Ride

In 1965 a group of Sydney University students investigated the level of discrimination against Aboriginal people that was being experienced in outback country towns in New South Wales.

Charles Perkins (1936-2000), who was a student at the University, led the Freedom Ride.

Charles Perkins came to prominence during these Freedom Rides and became one of Australia's distinguished Aboriginal leaders. He worked in the Australian Public Service and became head of the Department of Aboriginal Affairs in 1984.

The Freedom Riders were inspired by the Black protest movements in the United States where freedom rides were highlighting the level of segregation Black people experienced.

The university students found that in most country towns Aboriginal people were often refused service in shops and made to stand aside while others were being served. They were confined to their own section in movie houses, banned from clubs and pubs, and excluded from public swimming pools.

The Freedom Riders stirred up a lot of controversy across Australia. They were set upon by angry crowds and were placed under police protection.

Gurindji Walk Off

In the mid-1960s further protest took place in the Northern Territory when Gurindji stockmen and women walked off Wave Hill Station. This protest is regarded as an important event in the history of Aboriginal land rights in Australia.

Wave Hill was a cattle station owned by Lord Vestey, an English aristocrat. The Gurindji were protesting about their intolerable working conditions and poor wages.

In 1965 the Federal Arbitration Commission ruled that Aboriginal people working on cattle properties should be paid the same rate as other station hands. This ruling, however, did not take effect for three years.

The Gurindji were not prepared to wait. They went on strike and set up camp at Daguragu (Wattie Creek).

Soon after they petitioned the Governor General to grant them land there.

Integration Policy (1965-1972)

In 1965 the Commonwealth Government announced a policy of integration whereby Aboriginal people could openly express their cultural differences and give them greater control over their own destinies.

But the then Government did not do much to implement the policy and there was an overall lack of commitment to it. Hence change was slow, and the value of Aboriginal culture was still not acknowledged in mainstream society.

Commonwealth Referendum 1967

In 1967 a Commonwealth Referendum was held which allowed Aboriginal people for the first time to be counted as part of the Australian population. The change to the Constitution also allowed the Australian Government to legislate on behalf of all Aboriginal people.

The first census which included Aboriginal and Torres Strait Islander people took place in 1971.

The restrictive laws relating to Aboriginal Australians that had been in operation for over three decades were not abolished until a Labor Government under the Prime Ministership of Gough Whitlam came to power in 1972.

Soon after, under the Whitlam Government in 1972, a Department of Aboriginal Affairs was established with branches in every state and territory.

Chapter 6

Reclaiming Their Rights

1972 Self determination

When the Whitlam Labor Government came into power in 1972, there was a dramatic change in many policies affecting all Australians. Among these was the abolition of the White Australia Policy, and a new policy of self-determination for Aboriginal Australians.

The former Minister for Immigration in the Whitlam Government, the Hon. A.J. Grassby, said "When migration began here on January 26th 1788 all Australians were black and the first migrants were white…"

The new self-determination policy gave Aboriginal people the right to be involved in their own decision making. They had the right to manage their own communities.

This change in policy brought to an end the discriminatory laws relating to protection and assimilation.

The new policy of self-determination was to be administered through a new government department - the Department of Aboriginal Affairs (DAA).

When Gough Whitlam died aged 98 in 2014 a Gurindji elder, Michael George, said that Whitlam helped Aboriginal people get higher salaries, improved health, more education and better housing. He even helped the Gurindji get their land back.

The Tent Embassy

In that same year of 1972 on the lawns of Parliament House in Canberra, four activists erected the Aboriginal Tent Embassy to protest against the treatment of Aboriginal people in Australia.

A beach umbrella was erected on Australia Day - 26 January 1972, and a sign said Aboriginal Embassy. This was a political statement designed to highlight the fact that Aboriginal people were being treated like foreigners in their own country.

The Aboriginal Tent Embassy became a symbol of injustice to Aboriginal people.

Artwork by Marji Hill

There were various attempts to remove the Tent Embassy but it remained on the lawns of Parliament House until 1975. For many years the Embassy was set up at various locations around Canberra.

It became a symbol of injustice to Aboriginal people. In 1992 the Embassy was permanently re-established on its original site and it continues to this day to be a site of Aboriginal protest and a reminder of the issues that face Indigenous Australians.

By this time the new Parliament House had moved to Capital Hill in Canberra, so the Tent Embassy was positioned on the lawns of Old Parliament House.

In 1995 it was listed on the Australian Heritage Council's National Estate.

The Aboriginal Tent Embassy, a symbol of resistance and cultural revival, celebrated its fortieth anniversary in 2012.

Land Rights - Native Title

The 1970s saw a number of initiatives which led to the official recognition of Aboriginal land rights. Land rights are the rights of Aboriginal and Torres Strait Islander peoples to possess land and to have their original ownership of Australian land recognised.

In 1973 Mr. Justice Woodward of the Aboriginal Land Commission showed the way for a new approach to Aboriginal land rights when he delivered his first report. In 1974 he delivered his second report acknowledging Aboriginal Australian's connection to the land.

In 1975 the Australian Parliament passed the *Racial Discrimination Act*. This was designed to make sure that Australians from all backgrounds were to be treated equally and to receive the same opportunities.

There was also the establishment of the National Aboriginal and Islander Health Organisation, and the Gurindji in the Northern Territory received leasehold title to some of their traditional land.

In 1976 the Australian Federal Government passed its historic, first *Aboriginal Land Rights Act 1976* (NT). This recognised Aboriginal land rights in the Northern Territory and enabled Aboriginal people to claim rights to their land where this could be proven. In time Australian State governments passed their own land right's legislation.

Aboriginal people had vigorously fought and resisted the invasion of British settlers' attempts to take their land in the late 1700s and 1800s.

Colonial governors opened up land for settlement right across Australia and claimed the land in the name of the King of England. The British colonial governments decreed that any title or legal right to the land that Aboriginal people may have had in the past no longer existed.

Aboriginal people eventually tried to negotiate to be allowed to stay on or near their land. Many Aborigines worked for those who had taken their land. Finally, they began to take political action to have their original land rights recognised and to have their need for land granted.

In 1992 the High Court of Australia in the Mabo Case ruled that native title could continue if no deliberate act by a government had extinguished that title. Such an act might include giving full ownership of the land to a settler or building a school, or public buildings on the land.

In 1993, the Australian Government passed the *Native Title Act* spelling out the circumstances where native title might be said to persist and what people would have to do to prove that it did. This act was amended in 1998 making it harder for many Aboriginal groups to claim native title over their traditional lands.

The Mabo Case

In 1992 the High Court of Australia handed down a landmark decision in the Mabo v Queensland case - known as the Mabo case or the Mabo decision.

The decision handed down in the High Court on 3 June of that year changed the course of legal history in relation to land rights in Australia.

It was a turning point for the recognition of Aboriginal and Torres Strait Islander peoples' rights because the Mabo decision acknowledged their unique connection with the land.

The High Court of Australia in handing down the Mabo decision recognised that Australia prior to 1770 was not *terra nullius* and acknowledged the Meriam people's right to their land.

In 1982 a Torres Strait Islander called Eddie Mabo together with four other men had begun a court case to establish their traditional rights over Merian land in the Torres Strait. This action led to the High Court decision.

Prior to the Mabo case, the European legal view of Australia was that in 1788 the land was vacant. It belonged to no one. This was *terra nullius.*

The High Court of Australia overturned this belief and recognised that the people of Mer had owned their land prior to 1788 and that native title to Australian lands could have continued after 1788.

The Federal Government passed the Native Title Act 1993 - a law allowing Aboriginal people to make land claims under certain situations but not being able to make claims on freehold (i.e. privately owned) land.

A few years later in 1996 there was the Wik case. This involved a native title claim on land that included pastoral leases granted by the Queensland Government. The court found that pastoral leases did not give the pastoralist exclusive possession of the land and that native title was not necessarily extinguished.

Therefore, the granting of a pastoral lease did not necessarily extinguish native title. Native title could exist with the rights of the leaseholder.

Bringing Them Home

The decade of the 1990s was a time in which Aboriginal Australians had their status in society put in the spotlight. In 1991 the final report of the investigation of 99 Aboriginal and Torres Strait Islander people who died in custody was made public.

This Royal Commission into Aboriginal Deaths in Custody investigated allegations made in relation to the high number of deaths of Australian Aboriginal people in prison. This became an issue because just so many had died in gaol after having been arrested or convicted of offences.

In 1997 the *Bringing Them Home* report was tabled in the federal parliament and its details shocked the nation. This was a result of the inquiry into the separation of Aboriginal and Torres Strait Islander children from their families.

Under the law generations of children had been taken away from their families right up until the 1970s.

The report documented the forced removal of children. Its findings showed that this forced removal was in fact an act of genocide and was contrary to the United Nations Convention on Genocide that was ratified by Australia in 1949.

Reconciliation

Reconciliation Australia is a national organisation that builds and promotes reconciliation between Aboriginal and Non-Aboriginal Australians for the well-being of the Australian nation.

Reconciliation itself is the process of improving relations between Aboriginal and Non-Aboriginal Australians. It is about accepting and acknowledging that they have been treated badly and it supports measures that may help reverse the situation.

Reconciliation calls for a willingness to accept today's Australian people as the inheritors of a very long and ancient culture and tradition established by the first people, and that this should be shared with all other Australians.

At the same time reconciliation calls for their right of Aboriginal Australians to be keepers of their own traditional culture and to recognise their position in the nation as Australia's first people.

A Council for Reconciliation was set up in 1991 - its first Chairperson being Aboriginal leader, Patrick Dodson. Then in 1992 the Council for Aboriginal Reconciliation held its first meeting in Canberra.

In the Year 2000 Reconciliation Australia was established as an independent, not-for-profit organisation and in May that year approximately 300,000 people marched across the Harbour Bridge in support of it.

A major national event called Corroboree 2000, which was a landmark for reconciliation in Australia, honoured and celebrated the achievements of reconciliation over the preceeding 10 years. It also established the guidelines for the reconciliation process to continue beyond 2000.

While Reconciliation Australia was impacting the nation, the Sydney Olympics put Aboriginal and Torres Strait Islander identity and status into the world stage and did much to celebrate the traditions of Australia's first people.

Athlete, Cathy Freeman, went on not only to light the cauldron for the commencement of the Olympic Games but to win gold in the women's 400m.

National Reconciliation Week falls between 27 May and 3 June each year. It was first celebrated in 1996 aiming to give people across Australia the opportunity to focus on reconciliation between Aboriginal and Non-Aboriginal Australians.

NAIDOC

NAIDOC stands for National Aborigines and Islanders Day Observance Committee. Its origins stem back to the 1920s when various Aboriginal rights groups protested against the treatment of Aboriginal Australians.

Each year there is NAIDOC Week which is normally held in the first full week of July. During this time the history, culture and achievements of Aborigines and Torres Strait Islanders are recognised and celebrated.

A regressive era?

After the euphoria of the 2000 Sydney Olympics, Australian government policy under Liberal Prime Minister, John Howard, appeared to take a backward step.

First of all, in 2005 there was the dismantling of the Aboriginal and Torres Strait Islander Commission (ATSIC) which had been established to give Aborigines and Torres Strait Islanders some control over their affairs.

It had received criticism from Aboriginal and Non-Aboriginal critics alike, but its shutting down according to The Little Red Yellow Black Book "undermined the operation of important community programs in health, education and culture." ATSIC was replaced with a Commonwealth government-appointed advisory board.

In 2007 there was the Intervention. The Northern Territory Intervention was announced by Prime Minister John Howard and Indigenous Affairs Minister, Mal Brough. The Intervention policy was in response to the report *Little Children Are Sacred* which addressed allegations of rampant child sexual abuse and neglect in Northern Territory Aboriginal communities.

The Northern Territory National Emergency Response (commonly known as the Intervention) was controversial and heavily criticised. Its legislation included removing the permit system for access to Aboriginal land; abolishing the Community Development Employment Projects (CDEP); and, freezing 50% of welfare payments. The government could take Aboriginal land and could subject Aboriginal children to mandatory health checks.

The Intervention received political support from both sides of Parliament and its many opponents regarded it as an "invasion" and a regressive policy. It was strongly reminiscent of the draconian policies of the protectionist and assimilation years.

The Northern Territory National Emergency Response Act expired in 2012. But the Julia Gillard government extended it until 2022. A new name was given to it: *Stronger Futures in the Northern Territory Act*.

The Apology

The 1997 *Bringing Them Home* report which documented the forced removal of Aboriginal children from their families was handed down. Those people affected by these separations are known as "The Stolen Generations".

The dispossession of Aboriginal culture and almost genocide of Aboriginal people together with the story of "The Stolen Generations" marks a dark and unhappy chapter in Australian history.

On 13 February 2008, the Labor Australian Prime Minister, Kevin Rudd, made his opening speech to a newly elected Australian parliament. In his speech he made the Apology, apologising to all Aboriginal people and to the Stolen Generations in particular. He apologised for past laws and past policies that caused so much grief, suffering and loss.

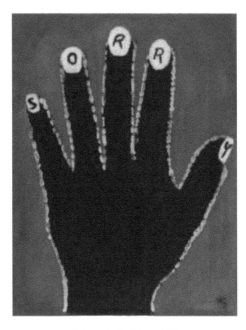

Art work by Marji Hill

The Stolen Generations are the many Aboriginal people who were removed as children from their families and communities by government officials, church groups and welfare bodies. The children were taken and placed in institutions or fostered or adopted into Non-Aboriginal families.

The day the Prime Minister said "Sorry" occurred more than 10 years after the release in 1997 of the *Bringing Them Home* report. This report documented some of the horrors and injustices experienced by the Stolen Generations. For many Aboriginal people the Apology ended a painful chapter in Australia's history.

The *Bringing Them Home* Report found that those children who had been removed from their families were at risk from different forms of abuse and that government welfare officials failed in their duty to protect children from this abuse.

The Report said that the Stolen Generations had their lives permanently scarred, and that the damage affected later generations of children and grandchildren.

It was concluded that between one in three and one in ten Aboriginal children were forcibly removed from their families and communities in the period from approximately 1910 and 1970.

A further conclusion of the *Bringing Them Home* Report was that, under international law since 1946, the policy of forcibly removing Aboriginal children from their families in Australia amounted to genocide - a crime against humanity.

Prior to this historic announcement, debate raged over whether it was appropriate for the Government to say Sorry. There was a groundswell of public opinion that the Government should say Sorry.

Thousands of signatures were collected in more than 400 'Sorry Books' that began circulating on the first National Sorry Day held in May 1998.

A National Sorry Day has been held each year since then.

The Stolen Generations lost their land, their culture, their language, their songs and their heritage. Subsequently, they felt they belonged neither to their Aboriginal heritage nor to white society.

The years of separation, sadness, and lost opportunities have meant that many Aboriginal people have not been able to operate very well in society.

They did not perform well at school, they found it hard to get employment, they suffered poor health. The disruption of family life and the loss of land and culture have sometimes led to depression, emotional distress, violence and excessive drinking.

Welcome To Country

Another significant event took place at that opening of Parliament when the Prime Minister said "Sorry". For the first time in Government history Aboriginal Australians performed a *Welcome to Country* ceremony.

The proceedings started with a Welcome to Country ceremony by Ngunnawal elders. A Welcome to Country ceremony allows traditional owners of a region to give their blessing for an event to take place on their land.

As a sign of respect, it is a simple acknowledgement of those past and present. If possible, it is done by a representative of the traditional owners; otherwise, it can be done by an appropriate speaker. Increasingly today a Welcome to Country forms part of official proceedings at public events.

Aboriginal and Torres Strait Islanders have proved that they are resilient. They have fought for their rights, renewed their cultural heritage, have received an apology for past wrongs. They step forth in reconciliation and are paving the way for a new future.

Aboriginal Health

From 1788 Australian Aboriginal cultures experienced the full brunt of British occupation of their lands, experiencing the dispossession of their cultures. What started in eastern Australia was repeated throughout the continent. There was no discussion with the first people, their lands were occupied, and tragedy continued to unfold.

Before the invasion by the British, Australia's first people had defined territories and knew the boundaries of their traditional lands. They knew its physical features, its geography, animals, birds, fish and plants. They looked after their lands and ritually cared for their country with ceremony, songs, stories and art.

But with the invasion and the taking over of traditional lands for farming, Australian Aboriginal cultures were almost destroyed. They fought to defend their country from the north to the south and from the east to the west. The Aboriginal population decreased with the killings and introduced European diseases.

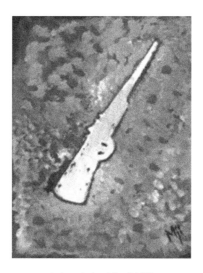

Artwork by Marji Hill

With the taking and occupation of ancestral lands most Aboriginal Australians were reduced to poverty and ill-health unknown before 1788. The "affluent" lifestyle of the past was over.

Before the British took over the lands, the lifestyle of the first people, their traditional access to the land, and its resources and their own traditional medicine, ensured that they were relatively free of the health problems that now beset them.

Aboriginal Australians have suffered extreme poor health since the British occupied traditional lands. Disease has been rife. Diseases experienced by Aboriginal Australians were almost unknown among Non-Aboriginal Australians.

Over the past three decades the government has tried various policies and programs to improve the poor level of health of Aboriginal Australians but the policies have failed.

While Canada, the United States and New Zealand have managed to lift the health standards in their Indigenous communities over the past few decades, Australia's Aboriginal people continue to experience bad health.

Australian Aboriginal health remains a national disgrace and an international embarrassment.

According to the Central Australian Aboriginal Congress:

Life expectancy is 20 years less than for non- Aboriginal Australians.

Life expectancy of Aboriginal people is considerably worse than for other comparable indigenous populations, such as the native peoples of United States and Canada, and the Maoris of Aotearoa.

Aboriginal boys born today have only a 45% chance of living to age 65 (81% for non-Aboriginal boys); Aboriginal girls have a 54% chance of living to age 65 (89% for non- Aboriginal girls).

Age standardised death rates for Aboriginal males are 2.8 times those for non-Aboriginal males; age standardised death rates for Aboriginal females are 3.3 times those for non-Aboriginal females.

Traditional medicine

Australia's first people had, and in many areas still have a traditional medical system. The extent to which traditional medicine is practiced varies widely amongst Aboriginal communities throughout Australia.

Illness and death are believed to be caused by sorcerers, spirits or ancestral beings. If a patient is ill and fails to respond to bush remedies a traditional healer is called in.

A traditional healer has special powers which may have been inherited or acquired through an apprenticeship. Their special powers which include strange or visionary experiences allows them to diagnose the cause of illnesses, cure these illnesses, tell the future, or protect someone against the evil powers of sorcery.

Sorcery is feared in Aboriginal Australia because a sorcerer can cause a person to become ill or die. Sorcerers can "point the bone" or capture a person's spirit with a bit of their hair, nail clipping or food. Bone pointing is widespread and involves short pieces of bone which can be used for deadly effect. Someone who is the victim of bone pointing eventually gets sick and dies unless a traditional healer can reverse the person's adverse condition.

When a person is sick a traditional healer promotes an atmosphere around the sick person which helps them regain faith and confidence. A healer helps a person's psychological welfare. The role of a traditional healer is a bit like a priest who instils faith, a bit like a Western doctor who cures the sick patient, and a bit like a coroner who tries to determine the cause of the misfortune.

A health initiative is taking place in Anangu Pitjintjatjara Yangkunjatjara (APY) country in the northern part of South Australia. Here there is a health care model designed to help traditional health care services work hand-in-hand with western medicine. Traditional health and medicine is alive and well in this region.

In Alice Springs in the Northern Territory the Akeyulerre Healing Centre is another example where traditional medical practitioners and healers are used in conjunction with traditional bush medicines to deliver health care.

Ailments like a toothache, aches and pains, bites and stings, constipation or diarrhoea are treated with bush remedies. But if the illness is of a more serious nature a traditional healer administers to the patient in a ritual manner which may involve massage, singing and the removal of "foreign objects" from the patient's body.

Once the spiritual or supernatural cause of the illness has been removed then it is possible for the sick person to get better.

To become a traditional healer here you are born into it and the process starts when a child is identified by both their family and community as having special healing qualities. The traditional knowledge is passed down through the family line.

Traditional healers work alongside Western doctors and health professionals attending to patients. "They deal with everything from childhood illnesses, pain relief, pain management to restoring the spirit balance within the body and treating loss of spirit".

But while there are exciting initiatives involving traditional healers in the delivery of health care in those areas where the traditional knowledge is alive and well, Australia still lags behind New Zealand and Canada where you can walk into a clinic and choose between seeing a Western doctor or a traditional healer.

In Africa and South America there are national associations of indigenous healing, recognised and funded by governments.

Over the past decade there has been some improvement in the health status of Aboriginal Australians but even in 2020 the government has failed to deliver the reforms needed to *Close the Gap*.

Aboriginal Australians remain the least healthy group in Australia's population. While the Australian Government addressed this disadvantage in 2008 there is still a long way to go.

- Infant mortality is almost double that of non-Indigenous children
- Indigenous Australians experience a higher death rate than non-Indigenous Australians
- there is an increase in youth suicide
- the unemployment rate is higher
- a higher level of Indigenous Australians are living below the poverty line

Constitutional recognition

In 2012 the Aboriginal and Torres Strait Islander Recognition Bill was passed in Parliament with support from both sides of parliament. The Constitution does not recognise that Aborigines have occupied this country for 65,000 years and that their culture is the oldest continuing civilisation on earth.

The Constitution as it is, allows discrimination based on a person's race.

The discussion surrounding constitutional reform and the recognition of Aboriginal and Torres Strait Islanders is controversial - some are for the change and others are not so sure. So, while there is strong support for a change in the constitution not all Aboriginal Australians support it. A referendum was planned but to date the plans for that are on the back burner.

The debate for and against can be found in the Creative Spirits website:
https://www.creativespirits.info/aboriginalculture/politics/constitutional-recognition-of-aboriginal-people

The way forward

While governments have implemented programs like the Intervention (now called *Stronger Futures*) and *Close the Gap*, evaluation of such measures demonstrates that these policies have failed.

The Castan Centre for Human Rights at Monash University in Melbourne argues that the programs have failed to meet their targets for reform.

In 2015 Prime Minister, Tony Abbot, is reported as saying the programs have been "profoundly disappointing". The targets to reduce the life expectancy gap, efforts to improve literacy and numeracy, and improving employment outcomes have not been on track.

In August 2020 the Morrison Government announced that it will provide a $46.5 million co-contribution over four years to build the capacity of the Aboriginal and Torres Strait Islander community-controlled service delivery sector.

Minister for Indigenous Australians, the Hon Ken Wyatt   said the funding is a significant contribution towards the priority reforms identified in a new Closing the Gap National Agreement.

The aim of this agreement on Closing the Gap is to enable Aboriginal and Torres Strait Islander people and governments to work together to overcome the inequality experienced by Aboriginal and Torres Strait Islander people.

The National Agreement has been developed in partnership between Australian governments and the Coalition of Aboriginal and Torres Strait Islander Peak Organisations (the Coalition of Peaks).

While the statistics point to the failure of past government programs and show that the health status of Aboriginal Australians remains a national disgrace and an international embarrassment, there are isolated pockets of positive development.

The body of Aboriginal and Torres Strait Islander leadership continues to grow. Neville Bonner, Marcia Langton, Mick Dodson, Pat Dodson, Charlie Perkins, Noel Pearson, Mick Gooda, Michael Anderson, Aden Ridgeway, Lowitja O'Donoghue, Ken Wyatt - there are too many to list. Leaders are emerging in politics, the arts, sport, medicine, law, education.

There are those leaders who distinguished themselves in sport and who have made an impact on the world stage: Cathy Freeman, Nova Peris, Evonne Goolagong Cawley, Adam Goodes, Lionel Rose, Michael Long, Eddie Gilbert, Ashley Barty.

Aboriginal Australia got world recognition after the mid-70s when the dot painting revolution took the world by storm.

Dot painting revolution

Artists experimented with colours, paints, brushes and canvas with whole new, innovative forms of expression and artists too joined the international stage - Emily Kame Kngwarreye, Minnie Pwerle, Dorothy Napangardi, Kathleen Petyarre, Gloria Petyarre, Rover Thomas, Clifford Possum Tjapaltjarri.

In 2011 Dr Chris Bourke, a dentist, was elected to the Australian Capital Territory (ACT) Legislative Assembly. He was the first Aboriginal Australian to complete a dental degree and he was the ACT's first Aboriginal Government Minister, taking on the portfolios of Aboriginal and Torres Strait Islander Affairs, Education and Training.

Nova Peris, former Olympian, became the first Aboriginal woman to enter federal parliament in 2013. That same year Adam Giles became Chief Minister in the Northern Territory government becoming the first Aboriginal person to head an Australian government.

In 2016 Linda Burney became first female Aboriginal Member of Parliament in the House of Representatives in Australia's history after claiming the Federal seat of Barton. At this election there were thirteen Aboriginal candidates running for election.

In 2019 Aboriginal federal minister, Ken Wyatt, was appointed as the first-ever Minister for Indigenous Australians in the Scott Morrison government.

Change is inevitable and the old will give way to the new. As more and more Aboriginal and Torres Strait Islanders make their mark contributing not only to their world, their communities but to Australia and the world as a whole, there will be an inevitable shift.

Aboriginal culture is not something of a bygone era. Aboriginal culture with all its variations is a living organism; it evolves, it adapts, and it changes.

It has been resilient in its need to survive. It steps forth in independence and reconciliation and paves the way for a new and fresh future.

The answer to health, education and social inequality lies with multiple factors. Communities must decide their own destinies.

Aboriginal and Torres Strait Islander enterprises must provide a viable, economic base; there needs to be recognition in the constitution, and individuals themselves must make positive choices for their own futures.

Aboriginal and Torres Strait Island cultures are continuing, evolving cultures.

Having occupied this continent for 65,000 years Aboriginal culture is the oldest continuing civilisation on earth.

SOURCES

The following sources have been consulted in the preparation of this manuscript.

Australian InFo International   *Australian Aboriginal Culture.*
   Canberra, Australian Government Publishing Service,1989.

Barlow, Alex   *Australian Aboriginal Religions.*   South
   Melbourne, Vic, Macmillan, 1994.

Barlow, Alex & Hill, Marji   *Art Of Arnhem Land.* South
   Melbourne, Vic, Macmillan, 1997. (Aboriginal Art)

Barlow, Alex & Hill, Marji   *Australian Aboriginal Stories.* Set of 7
   stories. 3rd ed. South Yarra, Vic, Macmillan, 2014.

Barlow, Alex & Hill, Marji   *Heroes of the Aboriginal Struggle.*
   South Melbourne, Vic, Macmillan, 1987.

Barlow, Alex & Hill, Marji   *The Land and the Dreaming:
   Aboriginal Religions.* South Melbourne, Vic, Macmillan,
   1987.

Barlow, Alex & Hill, Marji   *Art of Arnhem Land.* South
   Melbourne, Vic, Macmillan, 1997. (Aboriginal Art)

Barlow, Alex & Hill, Marji   *The Macmillan Encyclopaedia of
   Australia's Aboriginal People.* South Yarra, Vic, Macmillan,
   2000.

Barlow, Alex & Hill, Marji   *Rock Art.* South Melbourne, Vic,
   Macmillan, 1997. (Aboriginal Art)

Best, Ysola & Barlow, Alex   *Kombumerri: Saltwater People.*
   Port Melbourne, Vic., Heinemann, 1997.

Clayton, Iris & Barlow, Alex *Wiradjuri of the Rivers and Plains.* Port Melbourne, Vic., Heinemann, 1997.

Djandilnga, Elizabeth & Barlow, Alex *Yolngu of the Island Gailwin'ku.* Port Melbourne, Vic., Heinemann, 1997.

Flood, Sean *Mabo: A Symbol of Struggle: The Unfinished Quest for Voice Treaty Truth.* 4th ed. Kindle ebook.

Grassby, Al & Hill, Marji *Six Australian Battlefields.* Sydney, Angus & Robertson, 1988.

Hill, Marji *Saying Sorry to the Stolen Generations: The Apology.* Melbourne, Person Australia, 2009.

The *Little Red Yellow Black Book: An Introduction to Indigenous Australia.* 3rd ed. Canberra, Aboriginal Studies Press, 2012.

Lucas, Judy & Barlow, Alex *Wangkangurru of the Desert.* Port Melbourne, Vic., Heinemann, 1997.

Pascoe, Bruce *Dark Emu: Black Seeds: Agriculture or Accident.* Broome, Magabala, 2014.

Shnukal, Anna "Torres Strait Islanders" in Maximilian Brandle (ed.) *Multicultural Queensland 2001: 100 years, 100 Communities, A Century of Contributions.* Brisbane, The State of Queensland (Department of Premier and Cabinet), 2001.

Web Sources:

https://www.abs.gov.au

https://www.creativespirits.info/aboriginalculture/health/

https://www.creativespirits.info/aboriginalculture/history/aboriginal-history-timeline-1970-1999

https://www.creativespirits.info/aboriginalculture/politics/constitutional-recognition-of-aboriginal-people

http://www.australia.gov.au/about-australia/australian-story/reconciliation

http://www.crystalinks.com/mungoman.html

http://www.australiangeographic.com.au/blogs/on-this-day/2013/02/on-this-day-mungo-man-fossil-found/

http://australianmuseum.net.au/the-spread-of-people-to-australia

http://www.australia.gov.au/about-australia/australian-story/austn-indigenous-tools-and-technology

https://healthinfonet.ecu.edu.au/learn/cultural-ways/traditional-healing-and-medicine/

http://moreeinfo.com/lesson/historys/chapter7/7.1%20Changing%20Government%20policies%20Over%20Time.pdf

http://www.caac.org.au/aboriginal-health

https://www.theguardian.com/australia-news/2016/feb/08/northern-territory-intervention-fails-on-human-rights-and-closing-the-gap

http://nationalcongress.com.au/about-us/

Marji Hill - Author & Artist

All of her professional life, Marji Hill has been writing books to promote understanding between Aboriginal   and Non-Aboriginal Australians. She has fostered the spirit of Reconciliation in all her work since she was Research Fellow in Education at the Australian Institute of Aboriginal and Torres Strait Islander Studies (AIATSIS) in Canberra.

From 2008 to 2011, Marji was Deputy Chairperson of the Mosman Branch of Reconciliation Australia in Sydney.

After starting at AIATSIS in 1976 Marji, together with her late partner, Alex Barlow, produced more than sixty-five books on all aspects of Aboriginal Australia including the critical, annotated bibliography *Black Australia.*

In 1989 Marji was the Project Coordinator and one of the researchers and writers of *Australian Aboriginal Culture* the official Australian Government publication on Aboriginal Australians and Torres Strait Islanders.

In 1988 her work of non-fiction *Six Australian Battlefields*, which she co-authored with Al Grassby, was published by Angus and Robertson. A decade later it was re-published by Allen & Unwin as a paperback edition.

The 9 volume encyclopaedia, *Macmillan Encyclopaedia of Australia's Aboriginal Peoples* was published in 2000 and in 2009 she published *The Apology: Saying Sorry To The Stolen Generations.*

Marji has a Master of Arts specialising in Anthropology from the Australian National University.

She is a professional artist. One of her large oil paintings was included in the 2004-2005 Ballarat Fine Art Gallery Travelling Exhibition *Eureka Revisited: The Contest of Memories*. This exhibition travelled to Melbourne, Canberra and Ballarat - part of the 150-year celebration of the Eureka Stockade.

Another of her paintings hung for many years in the foyer of Jupiter's Casino in Townsville while her portrait of Jupiter Mosman, hangs in the World Centre at Charters Towers in North Queensland. These two paintings celebrate the story of Aboriginal boy, Jupiter Mosman, who discovered gold at Charters Towers in 1871.

Marji's paintings are held in many private collections in Australia and overseas. She is represented in collections at Ballarat Fine Art Gallery and the Catholic University.

As part of her professional work, Marji has travelled extensively throughout Aboriginal Australia and the Torres Strait.

Her maternal grandmother, Lucy Hauenschild, was an early Australian pioneer travelling as a small child with her family by wagon train from Melbourne to the Gulf Country in North Queensland.

Her early years were spent with Aboriginal people around her and after leaving Croydon in the early 1900s she eventually in the early 1900s went to live and marry on Thursday Island in the Torres Strait.

While Marji herself is not of Aboriginal descent she does have Aboriginal blood relatives living in Western Australia.

Marji Hill lives on the Gold Coast in Queensland and pursues her interests of writing, painting and internet marketing.

More Books by Marji Hill

Self-improvement:

Hill, Marji (2014) *Staying Young Growing Old.* Broadbeach, Qld, The Prison Tree Press.

Hill, Marji (2020) *How Big Is Your Why? An Author's Guide to Time Management and Productivity to Achieve Transformational Results.* Broadbeach, Qld, The Prison Tree Press.

Hill, Marji (2020) *A Create and Publish Toolbox: 101 Prompts In A Guided Journal To Help You Write, Self-publish, And Market Your Book On Amazon.* Broadbeach, Qld, The Prison Tree Press.

Aboriginal Australia:

Marji Hill (2018) *First People Then and Now: Australian Aboriginal Heroes of the Resistance.*   Broadbeach, Qld, The Prison Tree Press.

Ingram Content Group UK Ltd.
Milton Keynes UK
UKHW051433230523
422215UK00016B/98

9 780992 411831